Among the Lions

A Lamb in the Literary Jungle

by Harold Horwood

Among the Lions
A Lamb in the Literary Jungle

by Harold Horwood

killick press
an imprint of Creative Publishers
St. John's, Newfoundland
2000

Le Conseil des Arts | The Canada Council
du Canada | for the Arts

We acknowledge the support of The Canada Council for the Arts
for our publishing program.

We acknowledge the financial support of the Government of Canada
through the Book Publishing Industry Development Program (BPIDP)
for our publishing actvities.

∞ Printed on acid-free paper

Published by
KILLICK PRESS
an imprint of CREATIVE BOOK PUBLISHING
a division of 10366 Newfoundland Limited
a Robinson-Blackmore Printing & Publishing associated company
P.O. Box 8660, St. John's, Newfoundland A1B 3T7

FIRST EDITION
Typeset in 10.5 point New Baskerville

Printed in Canada by:
ROBINSON-BLACKMORE PRINTING & PUBLISHING
Canadian Cataloguing in Publication Data

Horwood, Harold, 1923-
Among the lions

Includes bibliographical references
ISBN 1-894294-25-4
1. Horwood, Harold, 1923-   2. Authors, Canadian (English) — 20th
century — Biography.*   3. Writer's Union of Canada — History.
I. Title

PS8515.04Z53   2000   C818'.5409   C00-950178-9
PR9199.3.H5954Z462   2000

To those who worked to found
The Writers' Union of Canada —
especially Graeme Gibson and Marian Engel,
without whom it might never have happened.

Preface

This second volume of memoirs covers a period during which I wrote and published twenty-six books. It includes an account of the early years of The Writers' Union of Canada, and brief critical biographies of some of those who worked with me to establish writing as a major cultural industry in this country.

—*H.H. Annapolis Royal, N.S.*
July, 2000

Chapter 1

The first time Farley Mowat poked his blunt, freckled nose into my office at *The Evening Telegram* in St. John's I was not much impressed. In 1956, while he was doing research for his books about deep sea tugboats, he had travelled by coastal ship along the south coast of Newfoundland interviewing men who had served the Foundation Company doing salvage work at sea.

"I'm Farley Mowat," he announced, and when that failed to raise an eyebrow he added, "the writer."

"Ha!" I said. "Another mainlander here to pick my brains." I'd recently had visits from two non-fiction writers with inflated reputations in Canada, who were now honouring Newfoundland with their attention. I didn't care much for these visits of the great and the near-great. I felt that if anyone was going to write about Newfoundland it ought to be me, not someone from the backwoods of Ontario or the mudslides of British Columbia.

"Actually," he said, "Jack Courage told me I ought to look you up. You know Courage. Speaker of the House of Assembly. I met him coming in on the *Bar Haven*. Do you drink rum?"

"Of course," I said. "You've got a bottle with you?"

"In my rented car."

"Then I'll knock off for the day and we'll go sample it. What kind of stuff do you write?"

"About the Arctic, mainly. And about the sea."

"The Arctic? ... Did you write a book called *People of the Deer*?"

Farley Mowatt

"That's me."

"Ah, now I place you. I was in the press gallery at Ottawa when they had that row about the tribe of Caribou Eskimos* the government said didn't exist. A few days later they flew in a load of buffalo meat because the nonexistent Eskimos were starving."

"That's the ones," he said. "The Ihalmiuit. I lived with them for a while."

"So we may have something in common. I've travelled a bit with the natives of Labrador as far north as people live along that coast."

That was the beginning of something too lasting and important to call friendship: a community of interests and causes, a mutual admiration society that has lasted, so far, for nearly half a century. Mowat and I have very diverse approaches to writing, and much less than a total commitment to the same crusades, but we are both sufficiently interested in saving the world from human folly, and its animals and plants from human greed, to give a strong common purpose to a major part of our writing. Our approaches are far apart. Farley usually speaks directly to a mass audience, as loudly as he can, writing books with mass appeal, and promoting them with numerous TV appearances. I have tried to appeal to a small circle of readers with tastes and interests close to my own, believing that if I can move them, their influence will reach out across the world and help to change it.

---

* At that time the name Inuit was rarely used, even by the people themselves, if they spoke with outsiders.

Farley and I have spent a lot of time in the same parts of Canada—in Newfoundland, Ontario, and Nova Scotia, where we have lived for short periods in each others' houses, and travelled and camped together without getting on each others' nerves. When we went sailing I shared his boat. I was the only Canadian present at his second marriage in rural Texas. His wife Claire is one of my few close friends, and a more faithful correspondent than Farley himself. She and I share a few special tastes, such as an interest in flowering plants and a fondness for baroque music.

The first summer of our acquaintance Farley and I went touring by car to some of the oldest European settlements in the New World—those in the great bays of Conception and Trinity that were settled by West Country fishermen in the sixteenth century, long before the first colonies were planted in what are now Canada and New England. He carried a tape recorder, collecting traditions from old people in Port de Grave and Ferryland, and a score of other places. I introduced him to dozens of Newfoundlanders whom I'd met in my travels as a feature writer. He and I have never been in competition. The kind of writing he does tries to be personal and emotional; mine tries to be factual and objective. We are sometimes able to use each others' research materials in complementary ways.

I soon discovered that he was an actor (and acting pretty nearly all the time), a salesman for his writing following the rule that you must sell yourself rather than your books—and at almost any cost, including your personal dignity. No posture seemed to be too outrageous so long as it would keep him in the public eye. I made some public appearances myself, of course, but they were low-keyed. I shrank from any kind of public posturing, and tended to stay out of the public view. I'd had quite enough of that in my years as a trade unionist and a politician. I preferred to write for TV rather than act for it, and indeed wrote about twenty TV scripts for documentaries that ran either half an hour or an hour. One or two of them even got to the Cannes film festival. The subjects had nothing to do with writing: the lives of the Innu people of Labrador, fishing on the Grand Banks, a celebration of the capelin scull, these were my subjects. Farley never wrote for the media, but made numerous personal appearances. After a quarter of a century of being one of Canada's favourite comedians, he came a bit closer to my point of view and said, "No more! I've acted the fool often enough." He continued to make TV appearances, to narrate films, to help sell his books and promote his favourite causes, but the days of clowning for the camera were over (more or less).

Farley is a very competent and very fast writer. His style strikes me as a bit florid, his metaphors sometimes extreme, his anecdotes often exaggerated beyond credibility, but the public is obviously in love with his stuff, even while the academics and a few lickspittle journalists sneer their jealousy. All his life, though, he has craved the kind of serious critical acclaim that he has rarely received. His books sell by the millions in practically all the civilized languages of the earth, but this isn't enough; he has always wanted the one thing he couldn't have—praise from the academic critics. He was actually hurt by the fact that he was never offered such a trivial honour as the Governor General's Award for non-fiction—an award that went, year after year, to some of the clumsiest, most badly written books in Canada. He also felt slighted because he was ignored in his home town of Trenton, Ontario. But great writers such as Margaret Laurence and Gwen MacEwen took Mowat very seriously indeed, said so in articles and in long broadcasts, and recognized that he was one of the major forces in Canadian culture. Margaret Atwood, in her early years, virtually idolized him. It wasn't enough. He wanted acceptance by the dried-up old prunes of the academic circuit, and this he never got.

* I visited Farley once or twice at Palgrave, Ontario, before he and his first wife, Frances, had become estranged. The house was hard to find, but the local postmistress gave me very specific directions. So I was not stopped by the big notice on the gate announcing that this was the property of the Keewatin Research Project, and underneath, in large red letters:

WARNING!
Radiation Hazard
dangerous to all
unprotected personnel.

This, he explained later, meant that without clothes you might get sunburn. The entrance was also decorated with a nude department store dummy. Beyond the mannequin everything was a thick belt of trees, beyond which Farley and his two boys were romping about completely unprotected in the solar radiation. Shortly after I arrived a female neighbour drove into the yard and enquired whether Frances had some eggs for her. "I have the neighbours well trained," he explained, and burst forth into song to the tune of *O Christmas Tree*: "*Au naturel, au naturel,* We love to dwell *au naturel.*"

Frances, however, was fully dressed. "You mustn't mind Farley," she said. "It's just his way. I've given up trying to civilize him." I learned a bit later that she had tried almost everything, including making one trip with him into the Arctic. Nothing worked. A year or two later they were living apart.

On another occasion Farley went cavorting along the cliff tops on a wild stretch of Newfoundland coastline wearing nothing but a pair of waders rolled down below his knees, red beard blowing in the wind. A crew of Irish-Newfoundland fishermen who passed by in a trap boat later reported that they had seen a spirit.

He introduced me to some of his Ontario friends—Max Braithwaite, Jack McClelland, June Callwood (all of whom I liked and admired). I even attended one party at Jack's house, a party that positively glittered with the *literati* and the *artistes* of Bohemian Toronto, and I was thoroughly bored and depressed by the whole thing, especially by the way they thought they had to work so hard at having a good time, at joshing and joking and entertaining one another. Years later Farley said to me, "The only party worth having is one that just happens."

Quite a few of them just happened at Beachy Cove and St. John's and Ferryland and Torbay when Farley and I were there together. He seemed to have a gift for drawing interesting people into his ambit, even those who had no connection with writing, illustrating or publishing.

We travelled together to almost all parts of Newfoundland that you could reach by car, and some of those you could only reach by boat. At that time I was editor and field assistant to wildlife biologist Les Tuck, and I was carrying my field glasses and my copy of Peterson wherever I went, so Farley resurrected his youthful enthusiasm for bird-watching; we searched for migrating shore birds on the tidal flats of the Southern Shore and St. George's Bay, were pleased to discover the resurgence of the golden plover (then believed to be near extinction) and saw such local rarities as Hudsonian godwits and black terns. We established for the first time that the sparrow hawk (now called a "kestrel") was not a rare stray, but a common resident of Newfoundland. We met—to our disgust—a team from the National Museum of Canada shooting every song bird in sight so they could stuff their skins into museum drawers. At a time when the bald eagle was supposed to be nearing extinction in Eastern North America because of DDT, we saw so many eagles on the southwest coast that a biologist employed by the provincial government felt compelled to explain to the press that what

Horwood and Mowat were seeing were not eagles at all, but ravens!

During one trip through central and western Newfoundland we lived in a tent, diluted our rum with water from wayside streams (something we wouldn't have dared to do on the mainland) and met just about all kinds of Newfoundlanders from conservative fishermen, the masters of trap crews, to wild backwoodsmen who seemed to live mainly by poaching salmon and game.

One of our more interesting encounters was at Barachois Brook, near St. George's, where Farley interviewed that grand old man Charlie Blanchard, then living in a cabin at Flat Bay Brook, acting occasionally as guide to anglers and hunters. By this time Farley had accumulated dozens if not hundreds of taped interviews covering everything from the arrival of John Guy's colonists in Conception Bay to a gory account of the Halifax explosion during the First World War.

At Barachois Brook we camped beside the road, entertained some of the local children, ate lobsters bought from fishermen at ridiculously low prices, and were involved in the great Barachois Brook robbery. This happened long after we had packed away our camp stove and retired to our sleeping bags replete with lobsters and rum. Some time before dawn car headlights came blazing through our tent. We turned over and half wakened, then drifted off again as the lights faded. When we got up to make breakfast Farley's suitcase, which contained only his tapes, tape recorder, and camera, was missing.

What to do? Talk with the local RCMP of course, and see if they might know a way to recover this priceless material, some of which otherwise might be abandoned in the woods as worthless.

"Think a reward might help?" Farley asked.

"Well, it might. But make it small. Something like ten dollars would be enough. I'll talk with some people around here and explain that the stuff in the suitcase belongs to a mainland writer who'll go away with a terrible impression of the people around here if his tapes aren't returned."

We waited a few hours, and then the policeman told us we could expect a visit from a local man.

"He didn't steal your suitcase," the policeman explained, "but it seems pretty certain that his brother did."

Sure enough, a rather scruffy-looking young man arrived with the suitcase. Everything inside was in order. He had found it on a path in the woods, he explained, and had taken it to the RCMP detachment, where the constable told him how to find the owner.

"Good," said Farley, handing over his ten-dollar bill, "and you tell your brother, next time he robs a car belonging to a mainlander, he should turn off his headlights first," at which the accomplice after the fact broke down in uncontrollable laughter.

"Now that," Farley said later, "was a policeman who really knew his job."

We had no further trouble during our stay among the Jakitars.* Word got around that we weren't your ordinary mainland sports, fair game for wily locals, but some kind of VIPs who shouldn't be molested.

We travelled the south coast on Farley's little ship, *Happy Adventure*, later celebrated in his book *The Boat Who Wouldn't Float*. There and elsewhere he blamed me for having wished this sinking derelict upon him, so I hereby put the record straight. I

---

* On the mainland, Jakitars are known as Métis. The origin of the word is in doubt, but Farley believes it is a corruption of a Basque word Jaiku-tar, which would mean "God's people" and that it comes from a time when these descendants of pre-colonial Europeans were the only non-pagans among Newfoundland natives.

did, indeed, suggest to him that the Southern Shore, especially around Fermeuse and Admiral's Cove, might be a good place to look for a small fishing boat that could be converted inexpensively for sailing. Next thing I knew Farley had gone to Admiral's Cove, where he bought a western boat, and took it to Trepassey to be refitted as a sailing auxiliary. I never saw the *Happy Adventure* until he already owned it.

Nor were the many sinkings recorded in his book in any sense the fault of the little ship. Farley, or somebody hired by him, was responsible in nearly every case. It wasn't the boat's fault that the stuffing box was improperly fastened when she was converted to a cruising yacht, so that she almost went down on her trial run. It wasn't the boat's fault that he moored her under the discharge pipe of a fish plant with her hatch open so that she filled with fishy effluent as soon as the plant started up. It wasn't the boat's fault that he left her in the water over winter at St. Pierre in the charge of happy-go-lucky natives, or that drift ice came in that year, punched a hole in her stern, and sent her to the bottom. It wasn't the boat's fault that he hauled her over on her side by a masthead at Burgeo, to scrape and paint her bottom, discovering later that he had hauled her down on a sharp, pointed rock, hidden by mud, so that she filled with water when the tide rose.

But it all made good copy. I joined him during his autumn cruising on the South Coast, to add my limited experience as a deep water sailor to his own, and help keep him from drowning himself. I had, after all, survived two voyages to Labrador in ships almost as small as his.

Farley had sailed from Trepassey with Jack McClelland, who was supposed to know something about the sea because he owned an expensive inboard runabout in Ontario, and had commanded a motor torpedo boat in the Second World War. Jack left Farley at St. Pierre (the place, incidentally, where he met Claire and they started living together on the *Happy Adventure*). I joined them there the next spring after the ship had been refloated and was being repaired. I joined him again that autumn at Hermitage, and sailed with him to some of the most isolated parts of Newfoundland's southwest coast.

The *Happy Adventure* was much smaller and rougher than my own cruising sloop, the *Fort Amadjuak*. She was barely adequate for two people. Small as she was at thirty feet overall, she had a schooner hull and was schooner rigged, had a diesel engine, and was fully decked, with an open cockpit aft. She didn't sail as well as the *Cutty Sark* or the *Bluenose*, partly perhaps because Farley had rerigged her by guess and by God, giving her enough sail to drive her along at six or seven knots, but not the careful placement of centres of effort that would have enabled her to sail close to the wind. She'd *point* into the wind, but wouldn't *go*. However, sailing on the beam, or winged out with a following breeze she did pretty well with her jib, jumbo, foresail and mainsail.

In those days no part of Bay d'Espoir was connected to Newfoundland's highway system, so we had a chance to explore in detail a part of the island that could be reached only by sea. Schooner sailing, we found, was a lost art among Newfoundlanders. No one could give us useful advice, so we felt our way, one at the tiller, one working the sails, which were stained as brown as mahogany from soaking in a bark pot, and sometimes streaked white with salt as we drove into the flying spume of that wild coastline.

We didn't do too badly. Perhaps because caution was necessary to our state of ignorance, we avoided any close brushes with Father Neptune. Nothing much happened while I was on board, but Farley had one bad scare while sailing through Lampoides Passage with Claire. This narrow canyon between thousand-foot cliffs follows an ancient geologic rift that buried a strip of mountain under 300 fathoms of water. The ship was running free with a wind of twenty miles an hour, sheets made fast and everything drawing, when a forty-mile gust swept down through a chimney in the cliffs, caught her on the beam, and laid her on her side before he could loose the main sheet. Water poured over the rail, sloshed across the cabin roof, and cascaded down an open hatch into the bilges. Only her built-in seaworthiness (and the half ton of outside ballast that I had persuaded Farley to have bolted to her keel) got her back in sailing trim. After that, he never made the main sheet fast again, but held it, as he sat at the tiller, with a turn around a tholepin.

The nearest we came to an emergency was in late September when we drove up Hermitage Bay with a stiff breeze astern. As the stiff breeze increased, and the masts began to bend, Farley wanted to take in sail, but I, perhaps a little intoxicated with the joy of sailing, wanted to see what she could do if pushed really hard. She soon reached her limit. As the wind increased, her spruce spars seemed to be bending like fishing rods. Farley insisted they were bending "at least twelve degrees" though I was convinced, myself, that they were not bending more than ten. Anyway, it was obvious that if the sail didn't blow out then the rigging or the mast could be expected to snap. Nothing remained but to turn into the wind and shorten sail. The job of doing this fell to my lot (as I well deserved) while Farley remained in comparative comfort and vast responsibility at the helm in the bone-dry cockpit. The nastiest part was standing out on the bobstay taking down the headsails while trying to hang on as the bowsprit dipped into every green comber, plunging me rhythmically into the near-freezing water. But even then there was some compensation in the thought that I was doing what my ancestors had done for hundreds of years, and that I might be the last Newfoundlander handling sails on a small ship in a storm.

As we lay at anchor that night with our kerosene lights aglow, discussing the passage over glasses of St. Pierre rum, it seemed well worth the hard work and the wetting.

Our journey took us into a land rarely seen outside history books. We had no modern gear; we sounded our way into uncharted bays and coves with a lead line, as Basque explorers had done on this coast almost five centuries before us. We entered a wilderness without human inhabitants, where the sky was ruled by soaring eagles, and the waters by cruising whales. We waded naked in the shallows of landlocked bays to collect shellfish, as the Beothuck Indians had done in the days before the Basques. We cooked blue mussels and clam chowders flavoured with chopped kelp, feasted on delicate scallops that paved the bottoms of the little coves, cooked fillets of pink ocean perch pulled from the deep trenches of Bay d'Espoir, and ate meals of monstrous moon snails dipped in buttered rum.

We collected the moon snails just off a long shallow point that separates Milltown and Conne River. A taggle of barefoot Mi'kmaq boys hiked out behind us to the point and watched fascinated as we plunged into the warm water of the bay, collecting snails. Finally the eldest, a boy of eleven or twelve, asked what we were going to do with them.

"We're going to cook them and eat them," I said.

"But..." the boy still seemed puzzled... "only Indians eat those things."

The fishermen of Richard's Harbour, who saw me cleaning and frying fillets of conners, were equally astonished.

"They're delicious," I said, "really a lot like trout. Want to try them?"

They laughed and shook their heads. No one with any sense had ever eaten a conner.

Besides Richard's Harbour, we visited McCallum, Pushthrough, Stone Valley, Round Harbour and Gaultois, all places where men still landed codfish and herring, some of it salted and dried on flakes. We also visited many harbours once populous, but now uninhabited—places such as the Three Goblins, Patrick's Harbour, and Barachois de Cerf.

We spent the month of September in a land where bald eagles soared constantly overhead; we counted forty-three of them. I had seen one or two eagles at various places in Newfoundland, but had never imagined that they could be found on every cliff top, or perched on trees at quarter-mile intervals along an entire coastline, but when we sailed through Little Passage, there they were: more eagles than herring gulls—and on one beach we found out why; an eagle stood on the rocks dismembering a herring gull; we also saw one that had killed a gannet.

Everywhere we went that autumn local people came to visit. Few had expected ever again to see a schooner under sail, even a very small one, for the schooner rig is rarely favoured by yachtsmen—the only people still under sail—and working schooners had all been converted to motor vessels, their rigs used only for hoisting freight. The two of us must have looked like music hall pirates—bronzed, barefoot, bearded to the eyes, a banner with a strange device floating from our masthead. Farley had been given this flag by a fisherman from Miquelon, a banner of the Basque Provinces with their intertwined crosses—not flown officially since the last Basque revolt against Spain ended with defeat in 1876. One Newfoundland coastal captain came on board to tell us that he had looked in vain for our insignia in his flag book, and wondered what on earth it meant.

We were sailing a coast that had been explored by the Basque in the sixteenth century, if not before, then explored again by Channel Islanders working for great Jersey merchant houses with branch plants in Newfoundland. In many a little cove now uninhabited we found traces of former occupation: roads built from carefully fitted stones now overgrown with trees, stone foundations of what had once been substantial buildings, bricks and roof tiles stamped with the insignia of Channel Island firms, used here to build shore bases for whaling crews that had hunted Bay d'Espoir in open boats.

At Head of the Bay we talked with people whose ancestors had been among the earliest English settlers, people whose great grandfathers had walked across the country from Notre Dame Bay, and settled down to fishing and logging. One of them was a man whose ancestor had hunted Beothucks on the Exploits River. In all likelihood Richard's Harbour was named for this famous Indian killer from Notre Dame Bay, Richard Richards, nicknamed "Double Dick," who, we learned from his descendants, had crossed the island and settled on this part of the south coast.

We also talked with Mi'kmaqs whose grandparents had preserved traditions of a strange tribe that never actually came out to the south coast, but whom they sometimes met on the headwaters of the rivers flowing into the bay, a century or a century and a half before then—people who still hunted with bows, and roasted their meat on sticks over open fires.

When we lay at anchor in Middle Goblin, the spookiest of the Three Goblins, where black forests seem to descend out of the sky into the sea, and there is really no holding ground for anchors, it was easy to understand why French fishermen of the seventeenth century had named this place Baie des Esprits—the Bay of Spirits. English-speaking Newfoundlanders later corrupted this to Bay Despair, and the Newfoundland government, in a mistaken effort at restoration, corrupted it still further to Bay d'Espoir, which in French would mean "Bay of Hope." We got to see the Bay of Spirits at almost the last possible moment. Within ten years of our first visit, highroads and power generation and a provincial park had turned Bay d'Espoir into just another collection of outports at the end of a long branch highway.

I joined Farley and Claire at St. Pierre in the summer of 1961, taking the ferry from Fortune. I brought my fifteen-foot canoe on deck, and in it went paddling into the harbour and up to the customs house.

"Mon Dieu!" some St. Pierrais exclaimed, as I climbed up the wharf. "Where are you from?"

"Oh, from Newfoundland," I said. So word got around that I had paddled across from the Burin Peninsula—fifteen miles of open ocean—in a canoe, and people came from all over to see the cockleshell that the mad, bearded barbarian had used to cross the strait. Such stuff is the birth of legends.

After ten days at St. Pierre I luckily received a cable asking me to return to St. John's. A lifesaver. The small French island with its ingrown feuds and jealousies (some of them dating from the Second World War) was beginning to get on my nerves. So I left Farley and Claire and their friends Jack and Lorraine Hermann (potters who were teaching a summer school class) to cope with St. Pierre, and headed back by ferry and car to Beachy Cove.

The Mowats joined me there later that summer and stayed more than a month while Farley wrote the final version of his juvenile novel, *The Black Joke*, and also the outline for an adult novel which Jack McClelland later talked him out of publishing. Claire, who had worked as a commercial artist in Toronto before meeting Farley, did illustrations for his juvenile novel, and later maps and decorations for one of his major works, *Westviking*, before deciding that she was really a writer, not an artist.

A year later they sailed the *Happy Adventure*, refloated and repaired after her sinking at St. Pierre, to Burgeo, where Farley bought a house and set a crew of carpenters to rebuilding it for them. They invited me to join them there that winter, so off I went by train and coastal boat through Port aux Basques to Burgeo, arriving just after Christmas while the mummers were making their rounds.

Though I was working on the fifth and final draft of my first novel, *Tomorrow Will Be Sunday*, and Farley on the early drafts of *Never Cry Wolf*, we had time for parties almost every night while the twelve days of Christmas lasted. The Mowats were on good terms with all the other "foreigners" living in the place—the doctors, husband and wife, who divided the southwest coast between them, the RCMP officer and his wife, the Lakes who owned and ran the fish plant, a district nurse nicknamed Scotty, and the formidable Mrs. Penney, matriarch of nearby Ramea, whose husband had been a senator. Farley also had friends among the fishermen. All of that would come to an end, bit by bit. Farley has always had a weakness for getting involved in the lives of the local people, wherever he happens to live. This leads to involvement in their local feuds and factions. In time, the Mowats became isolated, but in 1963 they were still at the honeymoon stage, and my stay there was very pleasant. Claire absolutely loved the place, including the most abominable winter weather south of Labrador. Of the many places they have lived, Burgeo was the only one where she was really contented, and she later celebrated it lavishly in her first book, *The Outport People*.

By this time Farley had given up trying to get me into Jack McClelland's "stable of writers." A bank manager at St. John's had made me a loan to enable me to finish the novel. At Farley's suggestion I had sent it to McClelland and Stewart. After a very long delay they had accepted it, and paid me an advance of $500. Then Jack McClelland had invited me to lunch, and explained the kind of revisions he thought it required. Take the sex out of it, he said, and write it as a straight growing-up-in-the-outports book. What he wanted, it seemed to me, was a sort of Newfoundland *Anne of Green Gables*. He also said that if I wanted to write about homosexuality, it should be something like *City of Night*, which I later read, discovering it to be a tiresome account of male street prostitution in an American city.

I didn't blame Jack for any of this. His job was to publish books that would help his firm escape bankruptcy. But the last thing I needed was Jack telling me which books to write. We parted amicably. I believed he was dead wrong about a lot of the advice he urged upon his writers. In spite of that he was the major force in Canadian publishing, then struggling to survive, and some years later I joined other writers in helping him to get the Molson Prize at a time when we believed he needed both the money and the psychological reassurance that the award would bring him.

Instead of agreeing to think the matter over I went straight to Doubleday and laid my manuscript on George Nelson's desk. As it turned out, they needed a Canadian book. Within a month I had received an acceptance, and the offer of an advance of $2,500, half of it in American funds, for separate but simultaneous publication in New York. Then George Nelson put me into the hands of a great New York editor who showed me how to add drama and "presence" to the book without altering its themes.

I repaid McClelland and Stewart the $500 advance, sending Jack a letter telling him that my puritan upbringing forbade me to keep money I hadn't earned. Besides the cheque from Doubleday, I had an equal amount of money from CBC scripts that I wrote that year—enough money, in fact, to buy a new car, a Comet (a mid-sized Ford, something between a compact and a full-grown Detroit monster).Three years after my plunge into poverty at Beachy Cove I was relatively affluent, though my affluence was very precarious indeed—I'd need some unforseen windfall to enable me to write another book without once more going into debt.

Farley was the first of many Canadian writers who became my personal friends. Soon I was deeply involved in cultural politics, helping to organize and run the Writers' Union of Canada, the Writers' Development Trust, and other such organizations. Margaret Laurence, Pierre Berton, Ray Smith, Margaret Atwood, Graeme Gibson, June Callwood and Marian Engel were among my associates. Indeed, just mentioning names is invidious. I could equally well mention John Metcalf, Silver Donald Cameron, Hélène Holden, Robert Harlow, and dozens of others.

Meanwhile I had moved to Beachy Cove from my native city, St. John's (for which I retain a deep affection) and have never lived in a city since then. Even in Ontario, where I spent the best parts of three years, I never lived closer than forty miles from Toronto, where the publishers had their offices. Beachy Cove became a sort of cultural Mecca, where famous people as diverse as Sharon Pollock and Glenn Gould came knocking on my door. The local media were never informed of those visits. Beachy Cove was a private place, not a public theatre.

Chapter 2

While working at the St. John's *Evening Telegram* as Joey Smallwood's principal opposition in the 1950s, I met four people who became vitally important to me as a writer. The first was the great naturalist Les Tuck (discussed in a previous book). The others, in addition to Farley, were Marguerite Reid and Tom Buck.

Marguerite was my long-term mistress, and to some degree my liberator; she provided some counterweight to the weight of my parents, which still tended to drag me down, and she encouraged me to break out of journalism at the same time that we shared book and bed during my first years at Beachy Cove.

Tom Buck, and his wife Helda and their children, came there to visit me, and later gave me most generous long-term support, a second home in Toronto, a house always open to me for weeks or even months at a stretch if needed, a second family in the all-important publishing capital of Canada. It is difficult for me to imagine what my life might have been like without them—much more difficult, that's for sure.

When I first met her in 1956 Marguerite was a stunningly glamorous woman, either honey-blond or redheaded as fancy dictated, pursuing a career as a freelance journalist, much in demand among the smart set in St. John's, habitué of all-night parties and bohemian circles. She followed conventional North American models: Hollywood, professional hair dressers, elaborate makeup, "mad, passionate" affairs, dances, expensive clothes, food, liquor. This, of course, could have been the end of me as a writer—such a life is for those who are always just on the verge of doing something, not those actually doing it, and of course it was remote from the world I had chosen for myself, and yet we discovered a comfortable fit, enjoying a relationship that lasted for nearly ten years. The fact that it didn't include a formal marriage was her choice, not mine.

Unlike my family, who were appalled by my decision to go off to the woods and write books ("throw away a brilliant career" as my father expressed it) Marguerite was wholly in favour of such a venture. By the 1960s I had already thrown away a brilliant career in the labour movement, and a promising, if somewhat less brilliant career in politics. To throw away a career in journalism seemed no more than a natural progression. Marguerite not only endorsed the idea; she helped me do it by joining in my search for a place to live at some distance from the city.

When I bought the first house I ever owned at Beachy Cove I was thirty-seven years old, at the decisive point where I had decided to stop drifting and begin living my life in my own way. Though I'd left a comfortable and prestigious job in 1958, I'd continued to drift—into a little freelance journalism, into a small venture at portrait photography (an idea invented by Malcolm McLaren, another former reporter, who had no gift for photography, but a gift for salesmanship), into founding and running *The Examiner*, a mildly socialist weekly—pulled and pushed into it by both McLaren and Ed Finn, the former managing editor of the *Western Star* who had resigned, along with the rest of the editorial staff, in protest against that paper's anti-union policy in the disastrous loggers' strike of 1959.

Abandoning the city was a truly symbolic act—a leaving behind of *all that*. I didn't go to the country experimentally, as Thoreau professed to have done—and indeed I had not read

Walden at that time. I went once and for all, in a lifelong commitment that has lasted, as I write this, for thirty-nine years. What I wanted was not something ex-urban, which I'd already experienced; but real wilderness. I had real wilderness at Beachy Cove for a few years, but ex-urbia gradually approached and swallowed the place up.

I first looked for land at the Goulds, about ten miles west of St. John's, near the place where I'd camped a year earlier when I first resigned from *The Telegram*. I preferred a place that could be approached only by boat, or by a footpath through the woods, a place to build a waterside cabin. I could find nothing for sale in such a location. Next I tried Topsail Pond and Three Island Pond, just beyond the city to the northwest, finding nothing suitable there, either. I toyed with the idea of going as far as Freshwater Bay, on the other side of the Southside Hills from St. John's. Again, anything I found there would have been approachable only by a footpath, but nothing there was for sale.

Then one day Marguerite, who had a habit of prowling around the suburbs in her car, said to me, "There's a little place for sale in Beachy Cove. If you like I'll take you there and we can look at it. It might suit you."

So we went for a look: two and a quarter acres of meadow, waist high with weeds, a few trees near the front, none anywhere else, a little house with boarded windows and four or five small rooms. But there were attractions: a view of a truly beautiful valley stretching eastward and northward to the sea, a range of rugged hills and bluff headlands reaching to Bauline, a far-off glimpse of Baccalieu Island like a battleship on the horizon, abandoned fields and patches of woodland on all sides. The nearest neighbours were perhaps two hundred yards away, separated by a rail fence. Hanging on the fence were three children watching our exploration of what had once been the property of their childless great aunt and great uncle. The little house had been empty without a buyer for over three years. As I was soon to learn, the asking price had dropped by stages from $4,000 to $2,500. A man named Littlejohn, nephew by marriage of the previous owners, was selling it. Now living in St. John's, he was willing to take a small down payment and forty monthly installments of $50 each, using the money to finance a new car. Perhaps even I could manage $50 a month.

The house didn't seem all that small to me. I was then living in one of my mother's apartments, with a sitting room about fourteen feet square, a minute kitchenette, and a bedroom in which there was just room to dress beside the bed. In the plain little crofter's cabin at Beachy Cove there was a large kitchen, two small bedrooms, small sitting and dining rooms, and a porch; also cupboards and an attic; by my standards, quite spacious.

Electric power did not reach the area for another five years, so there was no telephone, no plumbing, none of the modern conveniences that make such demands on your time—just five or six small houses within half a mile. The well didn't have a pump. Water would have to be drawn in buckets. But there was no worry about its quality; the house was on a ridge from which water flowed in two directions, to Beachy Cove and to St. Phillip's. Firewood was plentiful. You could cut it on Crown land at nearby Goat Cove, on places long since abandoned by absentee owners, and on patches of forest owned by the Parish of Portugal Cove, whose priest was generous in such matters. Even some private owners allowed neighbours to cut wood on their lots, which often extended to hundreds of acres, and had little or no use.

So I bought the place and began cutting down the weeds with a scythe, followed by a reel-type lawn mower (soon in the charge of neighbouring boys), brought a table and chairs from my place in St. John's, and moved in. I got a cast-iron kitchen stove from a junk dealer in the city, a bed from the same source, and a badly worn Persian rug, all for $70. 1 had an antique oil lamp that had belonged to my grandmother in the previous century. (I still have it.) I bought others for a dollar or two in the junk shops. Nowadays, all that stuff would sell as antiques at high prices. At that time it was almost worthless.

Marguerite was good moral backup. Even though I had not yet published a book she took my career seriously. She had talent and imagination, an urge to write short fiction. She lacked only the determination, the ability to survive disappointment, the ability to edit her material ruthlessly, all necessary for a freelance writer.

My friends at CBC expected my "back-to-the-land kick" to last a year at most. One of them asked if I planned to spend the rest of my life writing a few articles and the occasional media script. Marguerite believed I'd stay. And the neighbours were pleased. I was the first person who had arrived from the city intending to live there year-round. They did all they could to make the early months easy for me.

Marguerite didn't live at Beachy Cove full-time. Sometimes I wouldn't see her for several days, or even a week. Then she'd show up and stay for a while, bringing food and booze. She was at all times much more mistress than wife. She could cook, even cook well, but she rarely bothered. Once a year or so she'd outdo herself with roast beef and Yorkshire pudding and a dessert heavy with strawberries and brandy. As a general thing I did the housework. She took me to parties which I detested and to dances which I disliked. She loved pop music with Latin rhythms; she liked to play it on my battery-operated record player while we were in bed together; she thought it was sexy; I thought it was stupid. Her sexual habits were strictly according to the puritan standards of the time. I preferred sex outdoors in a private place under the trees and the sky. She preferred it in bed at night under the sheets, or perhaps in a sleeping bag, always in the missionary position. I suggested being a little more venturesome, but we always ended up doing it the same way as Saint Joseph and the Virgin Mary.

Occasionally we went on a pub crawl, and I remember one round of Christmas parties when she wore an absolutely outrageous dress fringed with plumes of vermillion red, making every other woman green with envy; she was the kind of woman who could get away with such clothes. We woke up next morning in bed with the outrageous dress in a heap on the floor. She never wore the thing again.

I still had to earn at least a skimpy living as a freelance writer, and I was sometimes out of the province for two or three weeks, seeing editors at CBC, *Maclean's*, *Weekend*, *The Imperial Oil Review*, scrabbling for a living in a market where almost no one ever managed to survive. And I wouldn't have, of course, except that my expenses were so low. I had no rent, no utility bills, a willingness to live at the same level as those on welfare. There were times when I could not meet the $50 monthly payment on the house. Then I borrowed the money either from my father or my aunt Lillian, but I was always able to repay the loans within two or three weeks.

I managed to get commissions for CBC scripts, sold some articles to the magazines, gave a series of fifteen-minute radio talks, even wrote some advertising for the Great Eastern Oil and Import Company at St. John's. A bit later I began collecting $15 a week for a nature column in *The Evening Telegram*.

After enjoying an income of $7,000 to $8,000 a year (which wasn't bad in the 1950s), I dropped below $2,000, and it must have been several years before I got up to $4,000. During that time I managed to keep my car—my only luxury. When it had to be replaced, several years later, I was able to give it away to a friend in need and buy a good used car from a dealer.

Those first years at Beachy Cove were a time of unmixed euphoria. My meagre income was no problem. I reached the point where I even sold the rocks from the old wall along the front of my property to help buy groceries (and later replaced them by hand, one at a time) but it never once occured to me that I was anything but the luckiest person in Newfoundland. I was not just happy. I knew it.

What did we have? The ancient kitchen range that could burn only wood, the bed I'd bought from the junk dealer, and a second one that had come with the house, old chairs, stacks of books, a little record player grinding out Vivaldi and Scarlatti and Prokofiev and Dave Brubeck. Clothes hardly mattered—old trousers, shirts made for lumberjacks, a pair of logans for winter, but in spring and summer I went barefoot, even when cutting firewood, as the neighbours told me they used to do when they were boys. Getting wood was a pleasure at the end of summer when the flies had ceased, and the days were pleasant but no longer hot. When I paused from woodcutting I'd go swimming in the Overfall Pool in Beachy Cove Brook, a quarter of a mile from my door.

That first autumn there were huge crops of berries, and plums from my own trees. The Reardons, my closest neighbours, helped me lay in wood. Without them, I would have had a cold time that year, but with their help the place danced with the heat, and was fragrant with the smell of wild berry preserves. I also had a hedge to prune, shade trees to plant, perennial flower borders to lay down, enriched with the well-composted materials from the privy. I put it all together in notes that filled my journal to overflowing, and became, a bit later, my first non-fiction book, *The Foxes of Beachy Cove*, which was a celebration of the land and its inhabitants, especially those in fur and feathers.

There were, of course, other aspects. The neighbours, and especially the neighbours' children, were perpetually underfoot. Friends from the city were often even more underfoot. They thought my life at Beachy Cove was one long holiday, and wanted to share it. Some of them even came calling around midnight, bringing bottles of whisky with them. It was a wonder that I managed to write anything that first year. But somehow I did manage, from time to time, to sink myself into the depths of a novel, and produced the first draft of *Tomorrow Will Be Sunday*. When you finish a first draft you never understand how far from finished a book is. If I could have forseen the five drafts that this book would require I would never have gone ahead with it. The neighbours were both helpful and exasperating. Beachy Cove was still an old-fashioned Newfoundland outport community where everyone's house was always open to everyone else, and there was a good deal of sharing—sharing work, sharing food, sharing beer and booze and home brew, sharing children (but not, despite my friend the Minister of Welfare, sharing wives*) and pitching in to help whenever you saw anyone tackling a major job. They borrowed a horse to help me get in my firewood, helped me put up a new rail fence, helped me harvest my first potatoes, and came visiting for long stretches whenever they had nothing better to do. Pete Reardon, my nearest neighbour, was the most helpful of all, but his two brothers, who worked as labourers on construction jobs, pitched in just as willingly whenever they were at home. A boy from just under the hill, Jim Antle, worked as hard as I did on digging, hauling and planting the poplars and willows that I set out for my first shade trees.

I helped in turn with their work, which was always much less than mine, shared the rare bottle of rum that I could afford, and above all drove them to the nearest bus stop, or the nearest

---

* Dr. Herbert Pottle. His phrase "Wives are exchanged like chattels" led to resignations in his department, and a libel suit which was later quietly dropped.

hospital, or the nearest bootlegger whenever they needed it, for none of them owned a car or was able to drive one, for that matter. Mine was the only transportation within half a mile or more. To the children, my house was simply their own, where they came whenever they wished, stayed for a meal, sometimes stayed overnight, as they would do with an aunt or uncle or cousin, and helped a lot with the work. I've never seen children since who could work so hard and willingly.

The men, too. They'd arrive with a dozen beer or a bottle of rum, and stay for dinner, and expect me to do the same at their houses. Whoever happened to be in your house at mealtime shared whatever food was ready to eat.

The women came to me only in emergencies, often medical trouble—urgent need to get to a hospital, radical first aid. I split one woman's fingernail right down to the quick with a razor blade, and took out a splinter that she'd driven all the way in. I gave her brother a capsule of oral penicillin one night in a blizzard when he showed up with an advanced case of blood poisoning, then bucked drifts to get him to a hospital. I drove another man to the clinic while his wife sat with him in the back seat, holding a pan into which he spewed blood from a perforated ulcer.

At first they all looked up to me. I was from another world—a world where people knew a great deal, a world like that of the village priest, but he lived more than a mile away, while I was next door. At the same time, I was on their own level, living a simple life like them, asking their advice sometimes, discussing such things as growing potatoes and getting in the firewood.

The men called me "Harold" like any man of their own age and class, but all the women and children called me "Mr. Horwood" and went on doing so, except the older boys, who gradually began treating me as a companion, like an older brother or cousin with whom they didn't have to be respectful or defensive.

Joe Harvey, the most literate fisherman in the area, one of the few men who could actually read, sang songs out of his childhood that I had never heard anywhere before, and have never heard since. He went pub-crawling with me at Torbay, and cooked up feasts at home. His three young sons came visiting, and took on such jobs as cleaving firewood, making kindling, weeding the garden, whitewashing the fence. I fed them on baked beans and slumgullion and whatever else I had in the pantry. When I started building a greenhouse the year after I arrived they did most of the building. When I finally got around to installing a septic tank those three (the eldest barely fourteen) did all the digging for the tank and the drain field by hand. To those kids such hard work seemed nothing worth mentioning. Years later the youngest of the three (to whom I'd given his first pair of skates, and also a new pair of boots when he had nothing fit to wear outside in winter) asked why I'd been so kind to them! He'd forgotten how much they had done for me, and remembered only that I had treated them as my own kids.

The most attractive of the children were two little girls with classic Irish good looks from the yard next door. They tagged after me like puppies as I worked around the yard, then visited almost daily after school. What could I do for them? Not much. Pet them a little, give them a treat if there was one in the house, take them to Bowring Park in the summer; there was nothing I could do to improve the shape of their lives, which held only the bleakest of prospects.

The boys were bolder, noisier, and more numerous. There'd often be five of them in the house at one time. None of them seemed to be afflicted with what my Aunt Lillian called "modesty." In a summer rainstorm they'd go out naked with cakes of soap to revel in suds and streaming water, then stand around

28

toasting themselves in front of my open fireplace. In winter they heated water on the stove and bathed in a wading pool, sometimes three together until the floor was wet with puddles and suds that they always mopped up afterwards. Instead of getting dressed the younger ones liked to dry off and run naked about the house where the temperature was usually around 80°F, playing wild animals, or wild Indians, or something of the sort.

Later, when I had a bathtub and they were a little older they'd come two at a time and ask permission to take a bath. In their own houses baths were with wash cloths and about a half gallon of water. One of the little girls told her brother that she'd like to share the tub, too, but she never got up the nerve to ask. There was almost as much puritanism in the lives of the girls as there was permissiveness in the lives of the boys, who, apart from carrying out an occasional order issued by their fathers, did just whatever they liked from the age of eight or nine onwards. They might occasionally get a few swats for some outrageous piece of behaviour, but they lived without rules, or made up their own within the peer group. In spite of this they were gentle, generally obedient, and never did any fighting. The only people I ever saw get into fights at Beachy Cove were grown men. But the boys were rowdy. The sort of game they loved was chasing each other up a ladder, across a roof, and down the other side, hollering as they went. Even though I loved them, I often found them hard to endure. The only time I could count on doing any writing was when the children were in school and the men were at work.

Jimmie Antle, a bit older than the others, would come and sit in my kitchen, and sit, and sit, and sit, like a visiting outport adult, saying nothing, until after an hour or so he'd say, "Well, time to go, I s'pose," then disappear without another word. He found a clump of rhubarb to grow in my garden, and helped me transplant the first trees—escapees from old yards on Witch Hazel Line. And his sister got permission from some relative to pick black currants from her bushes—currants I was more than glad to buy.

Two young Fitzgeralds, Kevin and Jerome from half a mile down the road, picked gallons of tiny wild strawberries, much better flavoured than domestic ones, and sold them to me for 25¢ a quart. I bottled them and used them in the winter to make strawberry ice cream.

I have a photo of Joey, eldest of the three Harveys, white-washing my fence like Tom Sawyer with bare feet and rolled-up trousers far too big for him—an old pair of mine, most likely. Many years later Joey found life unbearable and shot himself. A terrible shame he should come to it. As a boy he was gentle and full of good humour. As a young adult he was notably kind. Another boy who worked at my garden and woodpile eventually hanged himself in a prison cell. And there was a girl of fifteen or sixteen who jumped over a cliff because she was pregnant and unable to face her mother.

By the time the power lines reached Witch Hazel Ridge, and all the "comforts" of modern life were suddenly available, I had written my first novel, *Tomorrow Will Be Sunday*, by the light of flat wick oil lamps, with Marguerite leaning over my shoulder, and I had completed the first draft of *The Foxes of Beachy Cove* the same way. The dedication of my first book to her wasn't just a gesture. Despite her streak of puritanism, like being shocked if one of the kids walked into the room naked, she had done something to liberate me from my past and to help me get rid of the idea that sex was a somewhat sleazy activity. She also persuaded me that brandy and Benedictine were quite OK. But later on alcohol was one of the factors in her own downfall, though it seemed to do me no harm.

With the arrival of the power lines I switched to an electric typewriter, and installed electric heat in the house, but kept the wood-burning cookstove. I resisted until the last day I lived there the suggestion than I use an electric range, and despite the electric heaters, firewood remained our primary fuel.

We made other major changes. I built a stone chimney, and ripped out the wall separating living and dining rooms, giving me a large room with a stone fireplace at one end and a thousand books on shelves at the other. Above the fireplace I built a stone mantlepiece, and by sheer good luck the fireplace turned out to be an efficient heater. Everyone who ever sat in that room agreed that it was one of the most comfortable and attractive places they'd ever known.

Connected to the big kitchen by glass doors bought from a junk dealer we built a small greenhouse facing south. On sunny days in winter it provided more heat than the house could use, and we opened windows and doors. Flowers bloomed there all year, and I often worked at my typewriter in winter wearing shorts, basking in sunshine. By 1964, in fact, I had what must have been one of the first "passive solar" houses in Canada; the term wasn't current for at least another ten years.

If I could live any part of my life again, I'd choose those first years at Beachy Cove, while we were still driving over a one-lane dirt road that was often closed by snow in winter. How many people could say that some of the most rewarding years of their lives were the years when they reached the age of forty with little sign of success in their chosen careers? I was lucky, of course. For one thing I was still growing up. For another, this was the first peaceful, uncluttered, unhurried part of my life; it was a time when human, animal, and vegetable nature all contributed to my happiness.

Unlike the back-to-the-landers fifteen years later, I had no support from the government, or any kind of agency: no incentive grants, no unemployment insurance, no university backup, no welfare cheques, just a firm faith in myself. I was almost as much on my own as the Irish settlers were when they cleared the Beachy Cove fields in the previous century. What bits of cash income they had were from the sale of vegetables or hay or eggs or the like. What bits I had were from the sale of my writing, but most of my living came off the land, or out of the forest and the sea.

In 1962 I broke up a full acre of old grassland and planted it out. I grew potatoes, cabbages, beets, peas, parsnips, lettuce, cauliflower and Chinese cabbage. In that first greenhouse I grew tomatoes and cucumbers. With a scythe I cut paths through the weeds to the places along the fence line where stiles gave access to neighbouring property. One such path was a right-of-way from my front gate through Mick Reardon's back fields to the Ridge Path which had once been the main road from Portugal Cove to what was then Broad Cove (now St. Phillip's). Mick made sure I respected that right of way, and didn't close the fence at the styles. But the Ridge Path was largely overgrown. Today it is hard to find it, in places.

Jim Herder, boss at *The Evening Telegram*, gave me honeysuckle cuttings and climbing roses. I planted Oriental poppies, columbines, peonies and narcissus, divisions of roots from my mother's place in St. John's. Within a year the yard, and even the house, was filled with the perfume of flowers. The children mowed the grass on what served as a lawn.

A generation later it had all run back to weeds, but the maples I grew from seed were now handsome shade trees, the firs and spruces and poplars had formed a windbreak, the lilacs and roses were mature shrubs buried in blossoms in early summer, and among the weeds some of my perennial flowers were still blooming.

In my second year at Beachy Cove the neighbours to the south received as a gift the old horse they had borrowed the year before. He was named Prince, a beautiful black creature reputed to be thirty years old (he lived for another decade.) The owner had decided he should be retired with someone who would feed him and use him only for the lightest work. But he was still willing to haul a plough in ground already cultivated, to bring in light loads of firewood, and to carry boys around on his back without a saddle. The kids loved to ride him. Urged on with bare toes he'd obligingly get up to a slow canter. He liked people. Even in the last years of his life he'd wake up when you walked through his pasture at night, and come up to you to be stroked on the nose or scratched behind the ears.

Wood, of course, was plentiful and cost-free, produced by your own labour, and it didn't stink, like coal or oil. When every one of my neighbours in the late sixties "went modern" with oil stoves, I continued to burn wood. Thirty years later it is still the only fuel I burn for heat, except for a month in early spring when we sometimes go off on a trip to meet the sun coming over the Carolinas, and turn on an automatic oil furnace to keep the house from freezing while we are away. We now have a wood furnace, as well as a wood stove, and the only improvements we could imagine would be better models of both.

The wild land and sea produced masses of food: flatfish, cod, capelin that we cooked and smoked and put away for the winter, red currants, blueberries, raspberries, squashberries.* I never believed that sugar, used to preserve fruit, was in the least unhealthy, and neither did the kids who spent so much time at my house. Though I had little money in those first years I usually had plenty of food: home-baked beans with wieners, home-baked bread made from whole grains, home-grown vegetables, home-cured fish, dozens and dozens of crocks of jam.

---

* A delicious *Viburnum*, not high-bush cranberry, but vastly better. It grows poorly south of Newfoundland.

By the early sixties social assistance in Newfoundland was generous enough so there was no reason, aside from bad management, why children living in families that paid no rent, mortgages, or taxes should actually go hungry. And yet, some of the children who shared my meals went hungry at home, as they told me years later when they were adults, but I certainly didn't feed them out of any sense of duty or "charity": I fed them because I got so much pleasure out of their visits, and because I've always felt that food should be free to all comers.

Despite the poverty, the lack of even enough food, they were hardy and healthy kids. They never seemed to catch colds. While the last snow was melting out of the woods they went swimming in the pool below the waterfall in Beachy Cove River. One of those children, at the age of nine, completed the full twenty miles of the adult Oxfam walk. If this had happened in Toronto or Ottawa or Montreal the kid would have been interviewed on national TV and had his picture in the *Globe and Mail*. In Newfoundland nobody seemed to think it remarkable.

My closest relationshup with a child at this period was not with one of the neighbours, but with Robert Stacey, a small boy brought visiting from the city by a friend of mine. Robert had lost his father in infancy, was living with a mother and two older sisters, one of whom was an adult schizophrenic. Even his mother was on heavy doses of prescription drugs. By the age of seven or eight he was looking for a relationshup outside his family.

The day after he arrived at Beachy Cove he began referring to "our house" as though he owned it. He was the first child I'd ever known to stand and stare at the scenery in awestruck wonder. He wanted to do all the things you could do at Beachy Cove: go fishing, swim across lakes, learn to paddle a canoe. He was bright and intelligent and learned instantly, but was doing badly in school. That soon changed. I didn't tutor him at all, just gave him a quiet place to work, and his first incentive to succeed. In a single term he came up from twentieth to first place in his class. Many years later he graduated with degrees in both arts and social science.

It wasn't all easy or smooth. Perhaps for genetic reasons he suffered severe depressions when I couldn't even get him to speak except in monosyllables. But I set out to beat the odds: nutrition, B-vitamins, lack of stress. We had a far closer relationship than most fathers and sons, but at the same time he became independent. By the age of twelve or thirteen he decided on his own that the house needed painting, "took hold" as Newfoundlanders say, and did it, with neither help nor direction from me.

I dedicated my second book, *The Foxes of Beachy Cove*, to Robert, who, as I said in the dedication, "shared most of it." He continued to share my life until I moved away from Newfoundland in 1970, and continued to treat me as his father even when he became an adult.

Robert and Marguerite got along fine. She got along with *everybody*. But she was in no sense a surrogate mother. I can't think of their doing anything much for each other, or even much together—swimming, perhaps, a little boating; I tried to teach her to use a canoe, but she was really a city person, a visitor to the country, never fully at home there; I found to my amazement early in our relationship that she was actually afraid of the dark. In the city, of course, the nights were hardly even dim, and if she stepped outdoors at my place she wanted someone to hold her hand. I loved the dark, like velvet. And sometimes there were northern lights creeping ghostly across the sky.

In those days I was terribly intellectual. (I am still, but nowadays it's tempered with spiritual experience.) Everything had to be reduced to the logic of Newton and Einstein. Only later did I really appreciate what Blake meant when he talked of the "death" brought into the world by Newton. Then I got back to myth and magic and a mystery that was something more than merely the unexplained. I felt it, I suppose, even then, but I didn't believe it. So the universe knocks at your heart, waiting for admission. And Marguerite helped me open myself up to it.

But she was in the jazz era to stay, acting out its tragedies, constructing her own pipe dream, failing finally to hold back the night. She had a fine sense of the tragic in other people—perhaps an echo of the tragedy in herself. She could write a sensitive story alive with the human condition. Only the formal use of prose, the failure to pare it down and bring it within bounds, seemed to escape her. She was one of those who almost made it. How the fields are strewn with their corpses!

In 1967 she was suffering serious drug-related problems, doing uppers and downers every day of her life. She'd wake me at 4:00 A.M. and ask me to make tea, and with the tea she'd take a sedative, then, four or five hours later, her wake-up pill. She wasn't just on the upper-and-downer cycle like millions of other Americans and Canadians; she had progressed down the slippery slope to total dependency on habit-forming prescription drugs: how dependent, even her doctors didn't guess; she had two sets of prescriptions from different doctors and had them filled by different druggists.

That year we had planned to go to Expo,'67, and Robert was to go with us, but Marguerite was too ill to travel, so Robert went off alone to Montreal, and visited friends of mine in parts of Ontario—his first journey alone away from home. Marguerite and I spent our last full week together at the end of July, and it was almost the honeymoon over again.

Then, the evening of July 28, 1967, a stranger arrived at my gate in a car. He and Marguerite went and sat together in the vegetable garden, and talked for what seemed like hours. Then she came in and told me he had convinced her that she must go to town because her mother needed her.

She went. And of course I didn't believe her. An hour later, seething with jealousy, I went down to Portugal Cove, found a phone, and called her mother. She hadn't gone home. Mrs. Reid guessed what had happened, and invited me out for a drink, but I told her thanks, maybe another day. I went back to the house. A friend of ours arrived and found me pacing in the yard, unable to think about anything but the fact that Marguerite had gone off with another man. I wouldn't have believed I could feel so jealous and overwrought.

And that, essentially, was the end. I drove out to Port aux Basques to meet Robert on his return from Montreal, and we went on a fishing trip along the West Coast, where he caught a beautiful sea trout. Shortly after we returned to St. John's Marguerite went into hospital for a long stay, wound up on the psych ward, where they gave her insulin shock and heaven only knows what else, for months and months. When they released her she was forty pounds overweight, and sliding into the final twilight of her life. Five years later, after Corky was already living with me, Marguerite came to our house, and we spent an hour together. A few days later she committed suicide.

I owed her a great deal. She not only helped me to believe in my own vision, but she also saved me from herself. I would have plunged into a marriage that could only have been a disaster; she insisted on keeping the relationship at a level where it could be broken off, not without pain or tragedy, but at least without a mass of legal troubles. I felt guilty for a long time, though I knew the feeling was nonsense.

That should have been the end of it, but it was not. One evening in the dying days of 1999 I received a phone call from Winnipeg, the voice on the other end belonging to a woman I had never met.

"Did you know Marguerite Reid?" she asked.

"Sure. Very well."

"You dedicated a book to her." Long pause. "She was my mother—my *birth* mother." Another silence, then: "I think you're my birth father."

I knew I wasn't, of course. If Marguerite had borne a child during the time I knew her the child would never have been given up for adoption. But it turned out that this woman really was Marguerite's natural daughter, born in great secrecy at Halifax in 1956. She had hired a private detective, he had pointed to me, and she had located me on the internet, later getting some of my books out of the Winnipeg public library.

Shortly afterwards she visited me and my wife at Annapolis Royal, spent a week in St. John's, locating Marguerite's unmarked grave, and talking with people who knew her. With my help she even discovered the identity of her birth father, a visiting doctor who had spent three years in Newfoundland.

Did this contribute to the tragedy of her later life, the addiction to drugs and alcohol, the mental breakdown? It certainly seems possible. I still find it hard to understand why she never discussed the matter with me. I firmly believed that Marguerite was my last deep involvment. I was, after all, forty-four that autumn, and had tasted as much sex and marriage as I could want. Henceforth, I told myself, I would steer clear of such entanglements. I did, for some time. In the late sixties and early seventies a number of women, all much younger than I, offered to take up with me, and though with some of them I developed a warm friendship, I kept them at a distance. Little did I know myself.

I believed faithfully, as a child, that we were in the Time of the End, when the horsemen of the Apocalypse would ride through the earth, when the winepress would be trodden without the city, and blood would come out of the winepress even unto the bridles of the horses. Perhaps that is one reason why I have refused to believe in doom and disaster ever since.

When I went to Beachy Cove I was escaping into an immense affirmation of the glory and sweep of creative evolution, into the ecstasy of life's becoming. It is a vision I have never lost. Life's sorrows and troubles oppress me, sickness and infirmity plague me occasionally, failure of many kinds weighs me down, but behind it all I feel that I am part of a blossoming, an unfolding that is grand beyond the wildest leap of the imagination. This certainty within myself refuses to make room for nuclear war or the silly belief that the universe is running down like a clockwork toy because of some supposed law of thermodynamics. It was that knowledge I went to Beachy Cove to acquire—the peace, the certainty that lies behind accidents and appearances. I had enjoyed flashes of illumination at various times before, but it was at Beachy Cove, shovelling shit, cleaving firewood, climbing barefoot over the mountain, that it became not a brief illumination, but an arrived state of being plugged permanently into the main current of the universe.

The universe is greater than any of it parts, but every part, in a certain sense, contains the whole. Matter, life and spirit are continuous and indivisible. The agates on the beach are miraculous in the same sense as the field daisy or the falcon or the galactic cluster. At Beachy Cove I not only came to believe this—I came to feel it in my bones. Everything I touched became part of a universal miracle. I don't think I could ever have arrived at this state of consciousness in the city, or while working at a city job.

People have always given me trouble, though I've always felt they were well worth it. The neighbours who were so helpful were also nearly intolerable, making demands on me at the most difficult times. The children whose visits delighted me turned my house into Bedlam. I have never been able to resolve this conflict between the need for people and the need for solitude. At Beachy Cove the people gradually took over, and the solitude gradually disappeared.

Chapter 3

By the autumn of 1964 Farley Mowat and Claire Wheeler had decided to go to Mexico City, where Farley had arranged with a Mexican lawyer to get a divorce. His first wife Frances had declined to sue for divorce, and there were no grounds on which Farley could sue in Canada, where the government did not recognize marriage breakdown as a cause for divorce until years later. There was a "divorce factory" in Nuevo Laredo or some such place on the American border, where you could walk in at one end of a building with your marriage certificate and walk out the other with your divorce papers and decree absolute, but Farley wanted something that looked a little more official. Claire had her doubts in any case. She doubted that any Mexican divorce was legal in Canada, and wondered whether her Toronto friends would regard her as an adventuress living in sin. Her mother, who lived in downtown Toronto, had fewer doubts, and sent Claire a tearsheet from a magazine stating that marriage was going out of style; smart people nowadays were simply living together in free association. But Claire, who had always associated legal marriage with orange blossoms and old lace, continued to have her misgivings.

Sitting beside the blazing open hearth in my living room at Beachy Cove, Farley made this proposal:

"Why don't we drive—the three of us? We could take a month or two and visit some of the places we'd want to see anyway."

Farley didn't own a car, just a jeep, which would pull stumps if you were clearing land, but had limitations when touring. Claire had a tiny little Morris Minor, equally unsuitable for long-range travel.

"We could go in my new Comet," I suggested, and bit by bit we worked out the arrangements. We'd meet in Boston, where Farley wanted to discuss a book with his American editor. Then we'd visit friends of his in Connecticut, stop at New York City so I could make final in-house revisions to my novel with my Doubleday editor, make another stop in New Orleans where he had an invitation from his admirers, on to Florida to look for the grave where Claire's grandfather lay buried, and finally drive along the Gulf shore to Mexico.

It was a little more complicated than it sounds. They could fly to Boston, but I had to take my car, and we'd be leaving after Christmas, when the Newfoundland dirt highways were hardly to be trusted. A friend of mine, doing it the year before, had ended with his car perched in the branches of a big spruce tree. I'd have to get on and off rail ferries and make it on time to the Gulf ferry at Port aux Basques, then to still another one at Yarmouth. So I bought a ticket for a service called Car-go-Rail on Canadian National. They took my car at St. John's, and I met it on schedule three days later in Halifax. From there I drove to Yarmouth without incident except that for a few miles beyond Shelburne the road was buried under solid ice, requiring the most delicate touch on the steering wheel, and no braking whatsoever. Having got past this I checked into a bed-and-breakfast at Yarmouth, and next morning boarded the ferry to Bar Harbour, Maine.

Evening was coming on when we docked, and I began a very pleasant drive along America's oldest federal highway, US 1, with its chain of coastal towns and villages and pleasant sea-scapes touched by the setting sun. It was night when I reached the outskirts of Boston. I knew nothing about the city, had no route plan, but had been told that the address left by the Mowats was in Cambridge.

I couldn't follow route signs, but I could see from a road map that Cambridge lay to the southwest. Fortunately, it was a clear night with a good view of the brilliant Dog Star, Sirius, hanging over the roof tops to the south, so I reasoned that all I had to do was keep this star in view through my left-hand window. I did this as best I could for what I judged to be about ten miles, then stopped at a service station, and asked for the location of Cambridge, and the street where the Mowats had their hotel.

"You're *in* Cambridge," the service man told me. "If you drive down here for six blocks, turn right at the light and drive two blocks more, you'll find the street you're looking for." So with this incredible bit of beginner's luck in the most confusing city on the Atlantic coast, I arrived at the hotel where the Mowats were staying, ate at a nearby restaurant one of the worst meals I've ever been served—supposedly a grilled mackerel—and next day visited with them the offices of Little, Brown and Company, his American publishers, prestigious patrons of the Atlantic Monthly Press.

That afternoon Farley took the wheel of the Comet and found his way to Interstate 95—1 never knew how. We stopped next at a mansion occupied by friends of his in southern Connecticut, just north of metropolitan New York. They entertained us royally, fed us nobly the next morning, and waved us off to the city. For the first few miles everything went well, but the traffic into New York was horrendous, and we saw one side-swipe collision in the lane next to the one where we were driving. Both damaged cars kept going. There wasn't much else for them to do. To reach the Doubleday offices we had to struggle across Manhattan through miles of traffic jams. Farley and Claire found a mid-city motel at an outrageous price while I worked with my editor on final revisions for *Tomorrow Will Be Sunday.*

Early next morning we got away before the rush hour was at its worst, crossed New Jersey, and ere long were seeing green fields of winter wheat and rye, suggesting the sunny south. Next we saw our first broad-leafed evergreens, and by nightfall were well into North Carolina, where daffodils, pansies and winter aconite bloomed in the courtyard of our motel—a great change from Connecticut and New York, where everything was buried in snow.

We planned next to visit Claire's grandfather's grave in Pensacola. We arrived in the afternoon, and were promptly swallowed by an absolute jungle of urban sprawl: square miles of service stations, hot dog stands, "donut" joints and laundromats; it went on and on, seemingly forever. Claire hired a cab and went off somewhere—to city hall most likely—enquiring for the location of the graveyard where her grandfather had been buried beneath a marble slab. Nobody had ever heard of the place. No map showed its location. Somebody surmised that it had likely been built over during the real estate boom following the Second World War, but nobody could be sure. History, in Pensacola, reached back less than twenty years.

We escaped quickly into Alabama to a comfortable little motel on a sand beach beside Mobile Bay where we went swimming in warm Gulf water just before nightfall.

"Awfully cold, isn't it?" said the proprietor. "Nobody swims here before Easter." He guessed the water might be as low as 60°F. I told him that in Labrador I was used to swimming in water at least twenty degrees colder, but I don't think he believed me. The name "Labrador" had recently been added to the Newfoundland license plate, and everywhere we went people were impressed, as though we had come from Alaska.

Next day Farley and Claire visited fans in New Orleans. They owned an antebellum mansion that would have been at home in a Faulkner novel. Farley was upset when he discovered that I hadn't brought a necktie in anticipation of civilized dining. I pointed out that I didn't own a necktie, and had no wish to dine anywhere one was required. Perhaps he offered to loan me one; I don't remember, but in any case I made my excuses. This evening would be my only opportunity to paint the town red.

I went to an old restaurant in what I suppose was "the quarter" where there was a front entrance for whites and a side door for "coloured". I went in the coloured door, which led to a completely separate part of the building, and sat down at the counter. Every face in the place was some shade of brown.

"Excuse me, suh," said the black waiter, "but yo' come in the wrong doo'. This room fo' coloured people."

"I'm coloured," I said. "I'm a Canadian, and the people on my mother's side are Eskimos."

"Yo' sure don' look coloured to me, suh."

"In Canada," I said, "lots of coloured people have blond hair and blue eyes."

He was very uneasy about it, but he did take my order. I had delicious barbecued pork, the first time I'd eaten this southern specialty, and my first taste of pecan pie. Later I sat with a black man who had been eying me with amusement, both of us drinking orange wine. I'd never known such a drink existed, anywhere. But I was told coloured people drank it, even in cities of the north.

My companion, who had lived in Chicago, seemed to be the only person who wasn't embarrassed by my presence. He kept suggesting things I might do, and places I should visit, but of course I had only the one evening; otherwise I might have got a real taste of the famous night life of New Orleans. He was disappointed. He had looked forward to being my guide. Just then there was a campaign for integrated restaurants. Indeed, there had been a near riot during a street confrontation a day or two earlier in another southern town, but in this part of this most sophisticated American city racial segregation was still regarded as immutable.

Twenty years later I lined up at a supermarket checkout in South Carolina. Because they were short-handed, the white manager was operating a cash register. The customer in front of me was a black man.

"Will that be all, sir?" the manager asked as he checked out the order. There was no kind of emphasis on the word "sir." None whatever.

On February 7 we drove among flourishing banana plants out to the shore of the Gulf of Mexico, then past bayous and small farms through country where everyone we saw, blacks and whites, looked equally ragged and poor, many of the children without shoes. Just at dark we drove through an oil field where the air was rank with sulphur dioxide, and the flames of burning gas lit the landscape like a scene from Hieronymus Bosch. As we emerged from the smoke and fire we came to a small shack town named Sabine Pass, where we got beds in the local whorehouse, and met, in the bar, a lively group of Cajuns who were talkative and friendly, and eager to exchange information with people from their ancestors' distant home. They retained a tradition of their origins in Nova Scotia, and the wicked action of the English government in driving them from their homes to the distant Gulf. Among themselves they still spoke Cajun, which turned out to be old dialect French with many later intrusions. Since Claire had some command of modern French, she was able to talk with them a little in language they rarely heard outside their homes.

Next day we drove for many miles along hard sand beaches on the Texas barrier islands, and stopped at the Aransas Wildlife Refuge, which was famous for its vast flocks of wintering waterfowl, many of them from Canadian arctic nesting grounds. Here we had an unexpected bit of luck, when a small flock of whooping cranes passed directly overhead. These must have been just about all the whooping cranes remaining on earth in those days, and none of us had ever seen the rare and beautiful birds. We saw thousands of snow geese, numerous sandhill cranes, and a flock of wild turkeys that did not flush at our approach, but kept ahead of us on foot as we followed them through clearings in the woods. Except for the snow geese, those birds were all new to me, the first of hundreds of new species we saw on that trip.

Brownsville, Texas, is about as far south as you can get on the American mainland, right on the Mexican border, in the same latitude as Miami, and only about a hundred and fifty miles north of the Tropic of Cancer. Here we mingled with crowds of American sun-seekers, some of them having fled southward and eastward from the chilly weather in Arizona. They were shivering in shorts and thong sandals, still hoping to find tolerable temperatures without having to leave the good old USA, and bravely shopping for summer clothes, as though that might bring warm weather tomorrow.

We did not linger, but spent an hour or more explaining to Mexican customs officers what we expected to do in their country for the next two months. Farley was writing a book about Mexico (it never appeared). I was his research assistant, armed with notebooks and portable typewriter. Claire was his typist. No, we were not selling used clothing or other contraband. Yes, we had international car insurance, costing about ten times as much as insurance would cost at home. After much more of this we were finally allowed to proceed in spite of not having dropped a single hundred-peso note under the table. We drove off through a land of unrelieved bleakness, with a few scattered shacks among thorn bushes and scruffy cactus plants.

After many miles of desert inhabited only by hungry-looking natives, we arrived within sight of the Sierra Madre, where the villages began to show signs of prosperity, and such buildings as schools and town halls were almost splendidly modern, giving the impression of government affluence among private poverty. One school that we passed had two full teams of barefoot boys playing soccer, a gang of other children watching, a few men in colourful ponchos, and burros munching on scraps of vegetation. As we approached the mountains, streams running down from their crests provided a bit more irrigation, and we began to see the first scattered trees of a forest.

It was still daylight when we reached Cuidad Victoria, and found rooms with private baths at a place called the Florida Motel for a mere $2 each. Here I went to a store and tried my first words in Spanish by asking for a bottle of white rum. To my surprise, the language barrier was not a problem. But the rum, like most of the spirits we encountered in Mexico, was sailing under false colours. The labels everywhere were familiar, but the stuff inside tasted like slightly modified moonshine. The only spirits we found consistantly drinkable were the numerous brands of tequila, which proved to be fairly pleasant, especially if mixed with fresh coconut juice.

An English-speaking cab driver who had worked for years in the United States took us to an inexpensive restaurant where we were served the tender meat of a young goat and bottles of excellent beer—the one drink besides tequila that Mexicans seemed to know how to make. We had been warned not to drink the water, but our cab driver assured us that the water supply here came straight down from mountain peaks where there was absolutely no pollution, so we took the risk and got away with it.

We nowhere found the health hazards to be as serious as the American tourist literature made them out to be.

We went walking about the streets over elaborately tiled sidewalks, and saw young boys gleefully playing war games with naked machetes as sharp as razors. They seemed to be able to do this without danger. If any limbs had been lost, their owners had retired from the battle.

Next day we descended into the tropical valleys of central Mexico, where the vegetation became lush and exotic. Here coconuts hung high over the road, and brilliant flowering vines climbed the trees. We picked wild oranges, but they were both dry and sour. Indeed, neither then nor later did we encounter any edible wild fruit.

We stayed overnight at Quinta Chila, near Tamuzanchali, a lovely village with a few Spanish-Mexicans surrounded by tribes of native peoples. There we met a disillusioned young American, recently discharged from the army, who was trying to regain his humanity by hitchhiking through Mexico, and teaching every pet parrot he encountered to swear at the tourists: "Goddamn Gringo!" He was making excellent progress with a huge and gaudy macaw that lived on a perch in the courtyard of our motel. This intelligent bird had actually learned to say "gringo" but was not yet taking the name of the Lord in vain.

The weather next morning was unnaturally cold, and I went out wearing a sweater, but it didn't seem to bother the natives, dozens of whom passed along the roads, heading for market in only the thinnest white cotton. Few wore the tribal ponchos which would have provided some protection from the cold. Local boys, in even scantier dress, sat in a circle on the pavement playing a card game for coppers that were worth perhaps a twelfth of an American cent each.

We drove into the mountains and found the entrance to a cave that was mentioned in the tourist literature. Here we crawled on hands and knees through passages and into galleries that were full of bats, and—much to our astonishment—also held the remains of what seemed to be burnt offerings left by the natives. Were they the bones of chickens? Perhaps. Meant to pacify the evil spirits of the place? Most likely. Anyway, paganism here was by no means dead despite the efforts of Spanish priests during some four centuries. The cave had evolved its own small ecosystem of such specialized animals as white spiders, white cockroaches, white scorpions, all blind and adapted to life in the dark.

We drove up the mountain where a mad Englishman, many years before, had built an instant ruin, enormously more interesting and imaginative than Mackenzie King's ruins at Kingsmere. It included a crooked castle with flights of steps ending in mid-air, leaning towers that were sometimes bent, as well as far from vertical, pillars holding up nothing in the middle of a rushing stream, with a bridge that failed to span the water, among elements of nightmare.

To our further astonishment, we found that the local people had imitated some of the madman's themes. They had put crooked gazebos on top of their houses, and placed their windows at odd angles. On the crest of the mountain we found a conventional little village square, everything strictly vertical and horizontal, built by a local council that aspired to correctness, like the Spanish-Mexicans down in the valley.

A hundred miles or so north of Mexico City, at an elevation of more than eight thousand feet, we found an incredible Mexican spa (Mexican in the sense that Mexicans went there for holidays, and Americans passed it by). It was a fertile oasis in a really bleak desert, where hot mineralized water flowed abundantly out of the earth, filling swimming pools and private hot baths, feeding lush vegetation, and attracting dozens of species of exotic birds, all of it within less than a square mile.

The buildings in this elaborate resort were decorated with mosaics that looked Aztec to our uneducated eyes. The pavements were ornamented, and the walls of the baths were covered with handmade tiles in bright geometric patterns. All had been done, the owner told us, by native people using traditional designs. They must have worked at it for years. None of them, we discovered, could speak Spanish. At that time more than four million Mexicans spoke only the languages that had been current before the Spanish conquest, with no more than a few words of modern speech. They could greet you in Spanish, with warm smiles, but that was the limit of their conversation.

This spa had a big outdoor swimming pool with water at close to blood heat. My bedroom also had an attached private pool where you could swim a few strokes either way. It was all incredibly luxurious, like a villa that might have been built for the Emperor Hadrian when the Roman Empire was at its peak. The sun shone without ceasing. The only problem seemed to be the altitude. We stayed for several days, eating real Mexican food generously laced with red peppers, drinking real Mexican coffee, which had a slightly smoky flavour, and trying to identify the strange birds, but Claire never really adjusted to the thin air; she suffered headaches and debility. So we descended a couple of thousand feet to a part of the desert where she felt more comfortable.

At the old Toltec capital of Tula we climbed the largest pyramid in the region, and admired the grim monuments with their Aztec-like carvings and echoes of human sacrifice. We bought small copies of ancient idols, and later gave them to friends.

Then we drove to Mexico City, where we entered an inferno of haste, noise, and air pollution such as we had never imagined.

The whole city was smothered in a blue haze of fumes from low-grade gasoline; the sky was never really visible; the air was never really fit to breathe. Cars went screaming and clashing through the streets with horns honking, bashing fenders and bumpers, drivers swearing and shaking fists, frequently ending in wrecks at intersections. No wonder car insurance had gone through the roof.

All night the uproar continued, making sleep impossible. Then at the crack of dawn the cocks began to crow from their coops on the balconies of apartment buildings, crowded as they were with people and animals. We were stuck in this hellhole until February, when Farley got the necessary paperwork completed and paid the fees for his divorce.

We improved the time as best we could by visiting the great pyramids east of the city, commonly called pyramids of the sun and the moon, and were told by the cab driver that people in the next county were still eating dogs—a story we were to hear again, in other parts of the country, always concerning natives who lived some miles distant, across a state or county line. One restaurant we visited was jokingly called The Dog House.

On February 21 we thankfully left Mexico City behind us, and drove to the hideous little mountain town of San Miguel de Allende (an American tourist Mecca) but after one look around we descended into the eastern valleys and found a magnificent Mexican hotel about a hundred miles from the Gulf. Here I paid a mere twenty-five pesos a night for a spacious room with a bath, the use of a grand piano, and an interior courtyard with fountains and palm trees.

We then spent three days at a little resort named Mi Ranchito on the Atlantic slope above Vera Cruz, where we met an eighty-year-old woman, travelling alone on buses, secure in her advanced age and grandmotherly looks, carrying little besides her bird books and field glasses, determined to push her life list of bird species past the thousand mark before returning home. She introduced us to several birds we hadn't seen before, including one she called the squirrel cuckoo that I later failed to find in field guides. All told, Farley and I compiled a list of 167 species, mostly new birds from Mexico, not including many exotics that we could not identify. For all that, we spent only a minor part of our time bird watching.

The weather continued cloudy and cold. We weren't yet aware that this is normal for east-coast Mexico in winter, while cloudless sunny days continue for months and months along the Pacific shore. We saw thick pads of snow on the banana plants the morning we headed up toward the desert on our way to the Pacific.

On a beach just north of the small port city of Manzanillo we finally found what we wanted: cloudless days, warm sea water, lots of exotic birds and beasts, interesting neighbours. We rented a spacious beach cottage with two large bedrooms, two bathrooms, kitchen and sitting room for a mere $120 a month. The open air market in Manzanillo was a delight. It offered endless varieties of fresh food at ridiculously low prices—mangoes at 2¢ each, green coconuts at 6¢, red snapper at 15¢ a pound, and shrimp at 80¢.

Besides seven miles of public sand beach, there was a river and a lagoon with fish, turtles, roseate spoonbills and other large tropical birds, including parrots. On the shore of the lagoon there was never a soul in sight, except sometimes a naked young man in a pirogue, hunting turtles, or perhaps hoping for a crocodile, which had once been a common creature, but was now practically extinct.

On a beach just north of there we discovered at dead low water on a spring tide the protruding parts of a wreck, and learned that it was a sunken ship that had gone down with a cargo that included California gold in the days of the great gold rush. Because rip tides and streaming sand kept burying its bulwarks, no one had ever managed to excavate the wreck, only the smallest scraps of which were visible at spring low water.

This beach was also visited by man-eating sharks; we learned that a boy from a scout troop had been killed there by a shark only days before we arrived. This was in sharp contrast to Manzanillo Bay, which was believed to be perfectly safe because it was full of dolphins that kept the sharks far off shore.

We learned more about the wreck next day when we met members of an American salvage team who were trying to build a cofferdam and pump the sand out of the ship to get at the gold. They carried 30-30 rifles to defend "their" treasure ship against intruders, and assured us that while we prowled around the wreck they were hidden in the sand dunes, rifles at the ready, and "cheering for the sharks." Those treasure hunters were shadowed by Mexican gendarmes, but they had a DC-3 hidden on a nearby airstrip, planning to decamp with the gold if they recovered it, leaving the Mexicans in the lurch. We never did hear whether they found any gold, whether they escaped, or whether they rotted in one of the notorious Mexican jails.

About fifty miles to the north, following a one-lane sand track just passable by a car through the jungle, we visited the little first-nations village of Monzanilla. Here we found one Spanish-Mexican, a cheerful young man running an open-air café under a roof of palm thatch. He served fish freshly caught from the adjoining beach cooked on a stone stove over a fire of driftwood. The house shelters used by the villagers—hardly to be called houses—were of wattle and thatch, open to sun and wind. There was even a small church built of this material, not a real stick or stone used in its construction. The only local transport seemed to be by burro, and the only visitors to the beach, the day we were there, were local kids playing and swimming in the nude, as native children often did in western

Mexico. The jungle pressed in from every side, with monkeys in the trees, a jaguar always possible on the trails, and the occasional boa constrictor lying in the sun digesting a meal. We found such a snake on the road a few miles from the village. It was eight or nine feet long, with a large swelling in the middle, and seemed to be sound asleep. Farley and I examined it, and discussed taking it back to our beach cottage in the trunk of the car.

"You'll do nothing of the kind!" Claire insisted.

"Why?" I asked. "It's too small to do us any harm, and they make good pets."

"If that thing goes into the car I'm going to walk back," she declared.

So that settled the matter of the snake. We left it beside the road to digest the monkey or whatever it was it had swallowed.

A year or two later we heard that American developers had discovered the village of Monzanilla and had destroyed it, erecting tourist hotels, and inducing the government to build a motor road southward to the coast from the highway that runs through Guadalajara.

Near the town of Manzanillo (not to be confused with the village of Monzanilla) there were a number of little cabanas where you could eat and drink at very low prices, and dance to canned music if you chose. One place where Claire and I went dancing (Farley refusing) they had a tame coatimundi named Pussy. Another place served oysters from the adjoining lagoon, and bowls of delicious turtle stew. I hope we weren't helping to exterminate the remaining marine turtles which we saw alive on the dock waving flippers in the air, unable to turn themselves upright, hut I didn't think of that at the time. The drinks were mostly pulka, or occasionally tequila or mescal, all of it made from local cactus juices. You could also buy pulka on the street or the dock, served in tin cups at 2¢ a cup.

Local kids were friendly and obliging. They'd wash your car for whatever you chose to pay them, and would be pleased with the equivalent of a dime. They accompanied me across the tidal flats, and when I asked about the large seabird tracks that we happened to see, they not only identified them by signs as those of the white pelican, but took me to a place where we could see the big birds dozing in the sun. They were delighted by such simple things as looking through field glasses, and induced me to follow them home so they could share this pleasure with the toddlers in their family.

We met tourists too, of course, though not many at that season. One American couple were on their honeymoon, she celebrating her fifth marriage and he his third, but they had already filed for divorce, they told us, before they left the States, because she didn't get along well with the man's adult daughter. They had decided to have their honeymoon anyway, and seemed to be enjoying it. We also met one Canadian couple who didn't seem to be enjoying anything, but who shared a barbecue with us, and in defiance of their Jewish ancestors gobbled joints of pork grilled in a sand pit over an open fire.

At the end of March, after reluctantly leaving Manzanillo and driving through a desert no longer bleak, but now ablaze with cactus flowers, we arrived at Texarkana, a kind of Mexican annex to Texas, where we crossed into the Land of the Free, and found a county seat where Claire and Farley got married.

First a Wassermann test to insure they didn't have syphilis, which would make marriage illegal in Texas, then off to the chambers of Judge "Tip" Tipton, who was obviously excited to be splicing his first pair of Canadians, but who seemed to have trouble reading from the Baptist marriage manual.

"Ah'm new at this job," he apologized, "jest newly elected."

The bride wore slacks, and sneakers that had once been white. I can't remember whether the groom wore anything. A black man and woman, also waiting to be married, were brushed aside while the foreign VIPs blushed their way through the Southern Baptist vows. Along with a marriage certificate wreathed in the state's yellow roses, Claire received a gift from the county: a kit containing a marriage manual, a cookbook, a can of scouring powder and a bottle of aspirins. The newlyweds then boarded a train for Toronto.

Meanwhile I visited friends in Bowling Green, Kentucky, and was shown around the most depressed area of the coal mining region by Harry Caudill, author of *Night Comes to the Cumberlands*.

"Coal is a curse," Caudill assured me. "It brings nothing but misery to people unfortunate enough to live in its vicinity."

The hills here had been stripped of vegetation, the soil poisoned so it would no longer grow corn, the rivers polluted with sulphuric acid, the people left without employment or the means to make a living as their pioneer ancestors had done.

I next went to Battle Creek to visit my sister's family, spent a few days with editors in Toronto, and an evening with Angus Mowat in Port Hope. Then I drove on to Beachy Cove, which produced a week of warm May weather to welcome me home.

My cat, the big tabby tom with the paw mangled in a fox trap, was on the doorstep waiting for me, and made an unbelievable fuss over me for the next three days. After being self-supporting through the worst of the winter, he was still in good health, with no more than his usual good appetite. He even brought me a gift of a brown vole, thinking I might be ravenous after my long journey.

Chapter 4

A week or so after I got back from Mexico, CBC-TV offered me the chance to evolve from a mere writer into a TV personality, with the distant prospect that I might become as famous as the people who appeared regularly on Front Page Challenge. So here I was, with my first novel on press, and I could, if I wished, duck the difficult and demanding work of the creative writer in favour of the easy, glamorous work of the tube, demanding nothing more than a warm smile, a glib tongue, and the merest smattering of semi-literacy.

On May 4, 1965 a CBC producer offered me two contracts, one for a daily ten-minute interview show at $10,080 a year, and the other for a thirteen-week half-hour series at $100 a week. In 1965 a thousand dollars a month was a lot of money, and I was being offered $11,380 a year basic, before royalties, magazine fees, and anything else I could pick up on the side. It would easily amount to $15,000 a year, the salary, in those days, of a high-ranking civil servant or a university dean.

Of course I was tempted, but I didn't take time to think about the offer. I said "Sorry, I just won't have the time for it," and that was the end of the matter. The money was double or triple what I could expect to earn by writing books, but my experience at *The Telegram* had taught me that once I started doing regular work for TV I'd soon be doing it full-time. There's no quicker way for a writer to short-circuit himself than to accept such tempting offers from the associated fields of journalism and teaching, and especially, perhaps, electronic journalism, a profession requiring only the talents of a moderately good actor, and offering correspondingly great rewards in money, and even, I suppose, in self-esteem, because it must be easy to confuse your public image with reality.

Early in the summer of 1965 Tom and Helda Buck and their three kids, Carol, Lawrence and Daniel arrived from Toronto for a two-week visit to Beachy Cove. Tom had been news editor of *The Western Star* at Corner Brook until the IWA loggers' strike, when the editorial staff of the paper resigned in protest against the paper's policy of slanting the news as well as its editorial comment in favour of the employers. Subsequently he had been unable to find any work in Newfoundland, and had gone first to Montreal, then to Toronto, where he was now editor of a trade magazine. He had degrees in both chemical and electrical engineering, but was determined to work as a writer and editor rather than in his profession.

I had known Tom for some years before I left *The Telegram* in 1958, and had made one trip with him up country by canoe as far as the Annieopsquotch Mountains in southwest Newfoundland. He and Harvey Sheppard, of Little Rapids near Corner Brook, had gone in Harvey's eighteen-foot canoe, and I in my own fifteen-footer. Harvey had shot a moose, and I a caribou. Fortunately another party of hunters with a big boat helped us carry out the meat; otherwise it would have required two trips down Red Indian Lake to get it back to the logging road where I had left my car.

While we were camped near the headwaters of the lake on that expedition, Tom had used his electrical skills to rig a special antenna tuned to CBC Corner Brook, enabling us to pick up their signal with a tiny pocket radio and a set of headphones. While listening one night he suddenly burst out, "My God! The

Russians have put up the satellite!" This was North America's first public information that space travel was something more than a science fiction dream. There had been no advance news of the Soviet space program; Tom and I even had to explain to Harvey what a satellite was, and why it stayed up there. This was the most astonishing event since the bombing of Hiroshima, twenty years earlier.

Though Tom and I were never the very closest of friends, we shared many interests, ranging from science to wine-making, and he and Helda later became of enormous service to me in my writing career. They treated me with unfailing generosity during my numerous trips to Toronto in the 1960s and 1970s. After they moved out of the city to a renovated farmhouse near Great Rideau Lake, I always broke my trips to and from the nation's cultural capital in order to spend a day or two with them both going and coming. It was a considerable loss to me when they finally moved off to Hamilton in 1987.

Their first visit to Beachy Cove was memorable. It is hard to imagine in retrospect that five visitors managed to find room to sleep in that tiny house along with Robert and myself. But in fact we didn't seem crowded at all. I had fitted up one small room as a spare bedroom with double bunk beds that could sleep four people in comfort. Tom and Helda took the bottom bunk. The two boys shared the top one. Carol, in her early teens, had a daybed in the kitchen. Robert shared my bedroom. Marguerite simply stayed in town for the duration. After they went home Carol wrote me a letter in which she described Beachy Cove as "your paradise." I felt that way myself. I was happy there at all seasons.

The Bucks visited me again in December, and were astonished that the place was one great chorus of birdsong on Christmas Day. It was a year with a huge crop of ripe spruce seeds. Every morning when the sun shone (as it did most of the time that year) thousands of pine siskins and hundreds of redpolls sang from the surrounding trees.

Their visits were the beginning of a very long, close association. Helda gave me a key to her house in North York, in case I should stop by when nobody was at home. I could stay there any time I wanted, as long as I wished, and her place on Armour Boulevard became just as much home to me as my own house at Beachy Cove. After my first novel came out in 1966 with Toronto and New York publishers, it was of inestimable value to me to have a base in the city.

Over the next seven or eight years I must have divided my time almost equally between Ontario and Beachy Cove. Part of that time I lived at Farley's cabin near Brighton on Lake Ontario. For two winters I rented a small apartment in Schomberg, north of Toronto, in a house owned by Carol and Bernard Desoeur (Helda's daughter and son-in-law). But whenever I was in the city, my address was 410 Armour Boulevard. I even voted in that riding as a resident, and had the pleasure of voting for a black woman candidate against the axe-faced Mitchell Sharp, who was then finance minister. Tom, Helda and I all voted NDP.

Helda and I were the same age, within a few months, though from completely different backgrounds. She had lived from infancy in downtown Toronto, and told me she had learned to drive a car on King Street. She knew the city intimately—all its many attractions, and it didn't take her long to make me fond of Toronto, too. Even in St. John's I had never lived downtown, and only for a few years in the suburbs. I knew a little bit of Montreal—not much—and had visited New York. Apart from that, a great city was a new experience, and fortunately Toronto, at that time, was about the safest city in North America, where you could prowl by day or by night without the slightest danger.

With Helda as guide, I got to know Toronto in much the same way I had got to know and understand rural Newfoundland in my years of travel as a feature writer. I prowled through the slums, as well as through Rosedale, and along the Bridle Path. I went pub-crawling with residents of Logan Avenue, smoked pot in Rosedale, got high at parties in North York, spent hundreds of hours in parks and ravines and botanical gardens, bought incense at The Yellow Ford Truck, sat on a Yorkdale sidewalk with stoned hippies, took young people who were freaking out on drugs to a crisis centre, and drove them to out-of-town rock concerts.

We often visited the two great downtown markets, the malls above and below ground, the museums, the galleries, the science centre, the Toronto islands and Ontario Place. I saw squirrels drunk on fermenting cherries. A raccoon came out of a ravine at night, and allowed me to stroke its fur. Kids who didn't believe that strangers were dangerous came up to me and hugged me on the street. A beard had become a passport to juvenile hearts; if you looked remotely like Castro or Che Guevara you were accepted at once.

I spent days and weeks prowling alone through every part of the city. I knew the insides of the row of pawnshops on Church Street, the courts and parks of the high-rises on the outer fringes along Jane, the desert wastes of darkest Scarborough, the friendly neighbourhood businesses along the eastern stretch of the old Kingston highway—Danforth Avenue as it was called, the noisy Italian sidewalks westward along Queen, the insides and outsides of every shop and restaurant in Chinatown. In those days Toronto was "ethnic" enough to be fascinating, but not yet a Tower of Babel.

I loved the racial and economic mix—some people were poor, but not destitute, and a sense of joy and high spirits prevailed. I was privileged to watch Greek cooks preparing food in a restaurant kitchen that reeked of sheep fat and garlic, to see the inside of a Chinese noodle factory where everyone was white with flour, to play ball with Malays in a park, to take a group of boys through the greenhouse complex at Allan Gardens, where they wouldn't be allowed without a chaperone, to attend a rock concert under a meteor shower, and a folk festival with such groups as the Perth County Conspiracy. There was plenty of serious music, too, including visits by such great performers as Andres Segovia and Pink Floyd and Pablo Cassals. I loved lower Jarvis Street and the crowded, lively neighbourhoods of the racially integrated poor just east of there, where so many Newfoundlanders had come to roost. All of it was soon to be attacked by the developers, and to blossom with plastic pine trees and fake Victorian entranceways for the "inner city" set.

Living in Toronto within easy reach of Montreal and Ottawa allowed me to promote my books in the only way that seemed to matter in the late sixties and early seventies: non-stop appearances on TV and radio. In one week-long publicity binge I was on thirteen TV talk shows in Toronto, Montreal, Ottawa and Peterborough, with radio interviews in the major cities as well. The book I was then promoting was *Newfoundland*, published in 1969 by Macmillan (and still in print). It was a great opportunity not only to promote my own work, but to give a mass mainland audience some understanding of my province—a subject of which they were almost totally ignorant.

I could also talk face-to-face with editors of magazines and producers for CBC-TV. Out of such interviews came the occasional commission for a magazine article or a documentary for TV or radio, commissions that kept me solvent through the late sixties and early seventies. One of my greatest pieces of luck came when someone at *Reader's Digest* read *Newfoundland* and asked me to write a travel piece on the province. When they discovered that I could do an article of a set length that required very little editing they kept asking me to do others. I did travel articles not only on Newfoundland, but also Ontario and the Cape Breton Highlands, a whole series of dramatic rescue stories, mostly at sea; they sent me to the eastern Arctic, and to the north coast of British Columbia twice; they even offered to send me to China when I was researching a profile on Dr. Norman Bethune, but world travel was not one of my ambitions, and I decided I could complete the piece on Bethune without leaving Canada. To my amazement I found close associates of his who had never been interviewed by his biographers, and who had original information to contribute.

I also did sections for Reader's Digest Books—two on Newfoundland national parks, one on the Saint John River, one on the Upper Churchill. In all I must have done over thirty assignments during a period of fifteen years, and picked up from this source something like fifty thousand dollars with very little effort. I was able to do it without compromising my principles. I never pretended to endorse the politics or the social views of the magazine. The work was not arduous. I could do this kind of journalism in a tiny fraction of the time I spent writing my books or growing my gardens or exploring the country. It was far less taxing than part-time teaching—the resort of many writers—and it paid the expenses of most of my travel to places I would have wanted to go anyway. I got to see the Saint John River, for instance, all the way from the Maine border to the sea. I got to visit communities in northern Quebec and on the coast of British Columbia that I would never have seen otherwise. I got back to my old love, Labrador. The publisher paid for some of my commuting between Newfoundland and Nova Scotia and Montreal. They said I was "very reasonable about expenses," I suppose because I never tried to inflate my expense accounts.

I did other magazine pieces for *Star Weekly*, *Weekend*, *Maclean's*, *Imperial Oil Review*, *The Canadian*, *International Wildlife*, *Canadian Geographic*, *Atlantic Insight*, and even for an American sporting magazine whose name I've forgotten. Some of my magazine pieces were translated and published in Germany, Japan, Scandinavia, Italy, and possibly other places that I've forgotten. As Evelyn Waugh had said a generation before, the real reason for writing books is to get yourself into the lucrative magazine market.

I did several radio and TV "specials" an hour or even two hours long. Some of them, again, got me to places I would have wished to go anyway: to Northwest River and Davis Inlet in Labrador, to Quebec's North Shore of the Gulf of St. Lawrence, to the little towns of southern Nova Scotia, along Newfoundland's narrow gauge railway on the Trouter's Special. I did film documentaries for the TV series *Take Thirty*, and for a series called *Twenty-Twenty*, produced out of the regions. One of my most unusual commissions was for *CBC Wednesday Night*, the high-profile radio show of the time, to turn Farley's book, *The Serpent's Coil*, into a two-hour documentary. In the course of that assignment Doug Brophy (the producer) and I travelled far and wide in Atlantic Canada, including a visit to a tugboat attempting to refloat a freighter stranded in the lower St. Lawrence River. That documentary gave me my first detailed look at Nova Scotia, with visits to Sydney, Halifax, Wolfville, Chester, East River, Liverpool, Shelburne, Lunenburg and Bridgewater. It was an experience that probably influenced me, ten years later, to consider Nova Scotia as a place to live.

Except for the weather in April and May, I had no wish to leave Newfoundland, but working for editors and producers most of whom were in Montreal and Toronto had its problems—above all the three-day car-and-ferry journey to and from St. John's. I was doing an inordinate amount of driving, averaging well over 25,000 miles (40,000 km) a year. In some years I crossed Cabot Strait ten times—five return trips. Later, when I served on the Arts Advisory Panel and various juries for the

Canada Council, I commuted to Ottawa by plane, but airplanes were hardly the answer when you had to visit three or four different cities, and spend a month of short-range travel at your own expense. Plane tickets and cab fares would have been utterly beyond my means, but I could manage it by travelling in my own car. After I'd made a hundred trips across the Gulf I stopped counting.

Because I showed up so often by car, editors tended to believe I was one of those people who are afraid to fly. Actually I enjoyed what plane travel I could afford, or what someone else would pay for, and made numerous flights to all sorts of places in just about everything that could get off the ground. I flew in C-Bees, Cessnas, DC-3s, North Stars, Super-Constellations, Beechcraft, Norsemen, a Grummen-Goose, Beavers, Otters, an Auster Tri-Pacer, an unpressurized DC-4, a Canso flying boat, Vikings, Viscounts, Dash-7s and Dash-8s, airforce transports, numerous species of big passenger jets, and at least four different models of helicopters. So long as somebody would pay my way I'd fly anywhere, in anything. Paying for it myself was another matter. Even though I ran through twenty-two cars in my first fifty years of driving (most of them run right into the ground) the cost was far less than an equivalent amount of air travel.

When *Tomorrow Will Be Sunday* came out to an overwhelming reception by reviewers and feature writers at home and abroad, it was, of course, one of life's great experiences. A first book, especially when it is a big, mainline novel, is a great event in any writer's life—even if you are forty-two years old before it happens. But it was a disappointment, too. The Doubleday editors had led me to expect much more than I received. They had talked, for instance, of the Doubleday Award, which had gone to John Peter's first book the year before. If I remember rightly, it was $10,000, partly an outright prize, partly an advance against royalties on a second book—a lot of money in the sixties. I hadn't been *promised* the award, exactly, but I had been led to expect it. I also thought it possible that the book might get the Governor General's (I suppose everyone thinks of this possibility for his first novel, though it almost never happens, and in those days the GG wasn't worth much in either money or publicity). But there was a consolation prize: the Beta Sigma Phi award for a first Canadian novel. It provided $1000 which helped to tide me over until I could collect the advance on my next book. And *Tomorrow Will Be Sunday* did sell out its entire Canadian edition of 5,000 copies, without being remaindered or otherwise sacrificed. Published separately in New York, it was extensively and favourably reviewed in the American press. Doubleday told me it was a long time since any Canadian book of theirs had done so well in the United States. All this was very encouraging and stimulating.

Doubleday, who have always been considerate of their authors, sought my advice on paperback reprints, for which they had an offer or two, and turned them down because I thought the royalties too low, or the advances too meagre. Eventually, nearly ten years after the first edition, the book was reissued by Paperjacks at what I considered a fair return to the author and the original publisher.

Meanwhile, I had finished *The Foxes of Beachy Cove*. In this book I made use of some of the columns I'd written for *The Evening Telegram*, the Herders having returned to me the exclusive copyright to all my columns. I also used new material expanded out of my journal, and integrated the whole thing into a single story. I did the book in less than five weeks at the end of 1965 and the beginning of 1966, except for the illustrations, which I did in pen and ink, one each day for a month. There was an illustration for each chapter, but the publishers eventually decided to use only about half of them "to keep it from looking like a children's book."

Again I offered this book to McClelland and Stewart, and again Jack McClelland personally made the decision not to publish it, this time because he felt it would compete with one of "his" authors, Franklyn Russell, who had scored a modest success with *Watchers at the Pond*.

For the final rewrite of *Foxes* I rented an IBM typewriter, and at once decided that this was the machine for me. After a month's rental I signed a lease. When the lease expired, I bought it. When it began to age after fifteen years' hard use, I bought a later model, an IBM-2, and finally a third, which I'm still using today.

I carried that first IBM around with me in a suitcase like a portable. I used it on camping trips across Canada (plugged into electric outlets intended for trailers and set up on a card table in a tent), back and forth across the United States, and in a ship on the coast of Labrador, with a transformer to convert the ship's power from 30 to 120 volts. Even after I got the second machine I kept the first one as a spare, though it was now more than twenty years old. Farley, permanently wedded to old mechanical typewriters that were state of the art before the Second World War, has made great sport of my addiction to electronics, and especially to a machine that would correct its errors, if you caught them in time. Eventually some corporation gave him a word processor so they could take his picture with it for publicity, but he never used it himself. He passed it along to the typist who processes his manuscripts.

He continued to be very supportive, particularly in the use of the cabin which he had purchased from his mother on the lakeshore between Brighton and Carrying Place in eastern Ontario, a fine place, as it turned out, to work, and one that he rarely used except for a few weeks in early spring or autumn. I used it in midsummer when the inside temperature often reached 100°F, but I worked outside when the flies were not too plentiful, and in any case I have always had a fair tolerance for heat.

I transplanted a lot of trees and renovated flower borders that had not been touched for years, but the principal contribution I made to the Mowat place was to insulate it and get the oil stove back into working order so it would be possible for Farley to escape to the cabin even in mid-winter if he wanted to work without interruption. He and I both did a lot of writing (though never at the same time) in that cabin.

While I was there Tom and Helda and their kids would sometimes come out for the weekend. Occasionally, Margaret Laurence stayed there. Various friends of mine from St. John's stayed there too. Altogether, it got a lot of use, and may have been instrumental in Tom Buck's decision to take early retirement and buy the old farm at Portland on the Rideau waterway, an hour and a half south of Ottawa.

Between the Bucks and the Mowats I got generous help with the early stages of my career. Farley was even responsible for my being asked to write my third book, *Newfoundland*. He had turned down the opportunity to write it himself, feeling less than qualified to do it, and told them I was the only person who could do it properly. Macmillan's editors had never heard of me, but after looking at *Tomorrow Will Be Sunday* they decided that very likely I could manage. I grabbed the opportunity, and wrote the book in exactly one month, revising and rewriting each chapter as I went along. I literally had a filing cabinet already full of articles on Newfoundland, but I used none of it except for reference. I wrote the book as a series of journeys—by car across the island, by car over the major routes on the east coast peninsulas, by coastal ship along the south coast and to Labrador, working into the text the history of the province, and the rich anecdotal material that lay at hand in my files.

Macmillan paid only a small advance, $1000, but even if that had been the end of the matter I would have been paid for the thirty days' work I put into it. They had told me they intended to keep the books of their travel series in print for fifteen years; they anticipated a long-term sale. As a matter of fact, they have kept that one in print for a quarter of a century, first in boards, then in quality paperback. Though much of its information is now dated, it is still the most useful general book on Newfoundland, and I continue to get mail from people who have consulted it in libraries. If it goes out of print while I'm still working I'd be tempted to do a rewrite.

Long before *Newfoundland* was started I was writing a second novel. My editors, like almost everyone else, assumed that *Tomorrow Will Be Sunday* was an autobiographical book. Even Farley (who should have known better) assumed that it was. Had it been so, it might have been doubtful whether I could write real fiction or not. The one-book author was almost a Canadian institution. When I explained to my Canadian editor, Doug Gibson, that I had never lived in a Newfoundland outport, that the book was deliberately written to look like autobiographical fiction, while really being based on stories that I had heard from my father and my sister-in-law, he was impressed.

"I grew up in the city," I told him. "I'm the son of a business manager, not a fisherman. I never knew anybody remotely resembling Brother John or Christopher. Joshua Markady is based, in a general way, on my grandfather and my great uncle, and if I relate personally to anyone in the book, it is Christopher, certainly not Eli."

"That being so," he said, "you should write nothing but fiction for the rest of your life."

71

So I decided to have a try. I plotted my second novel to be set in St. John's, and I decided to create a moral dilemma of agonizing proportions, centred on the character of the prison guard who had befriended Christopher in *Tomorrow Will Be Sunday*. The theme would involve the then controversial subject of capital punishment.

My knowledge of the prison was limited to visits I had made while Member of the House of Assembly for Labrador. An old man who had been involved in a mercy killing, and who was convinced he was going to hang, had impressed me very deeply. I also remembered the last time the death penalty had been carried out in Newfoundland in 1942, when the authorities had decided, despite a public outcry for mercy, to proceed with hanging a respectable young man who had committed a crime of passion.

All these elements centring on the superintendent or the attorney general, and the question of sacrificing either his career or his conscience, seemed to provide the mixture for a good mainline novel. I worked on it off and on for a year. *One Door Into Darkness* was to be a novel about human damnation, just as my first novel was about salvation. It didn't come easily. At no point did the book begin to move of itself. At no point did the characters begin to take charge of it, as had happened in *Tomorrow Will Be Sunday*. And then it appeared that the whole question of capital punishment in Canada would become passé by legislation. A novel about the death penalty and the moral dilemmas surrounding it, a novel in which a hanging would take place at some point, would be a curious anachronism if published shortly after the death penalty had been abolished.

So I used the first draft of my second novel* to light the fire

* My third if you include a juvenile adventure novel that I completed and destroyed in the 1940s.

in my kitchen stove. A sacrifice? I suppose. But I had to be professional about my writing. It had to make a living for me. Though I made false starts on a few other stories, I never went very far with them. *One Door Into Darkness* was the only large piece of adult writing that I ever destroyed.

Meanwhile, I had long since begun work on a book that was not published for more than twenty years after I had completed a first draft—forty years after I wrote the first long passages. The book turned out to be my third novel and fourth book of fiction, *Remembering Summer*. In those days its working title was *To Toslow We'll Go*. It was the story of a symbolic journey, a journey through interior landscapes in search of salvation and escape from the horrors of society in our time. I picked it up and worked at it and put it down again throughout the first twenty years of my writing career, never being satisfied with it. It went through more drafts and rewrites than anything else I ever attempted, certainly more than I can remember. But my faith in the book was never shaken in the least. It remained my favourite project throughout a period when I wrote and published fifteen other books, including a novel of a traditional cast, which *Remembering Summer* most certainly was not.

I learned dramatic writing while doing *Tomorrow Will Be Sunday*. I learned the art of pruning non-fiction and shaping it into a coherent story while writing *The Foxes of Beachy Cove*. There were no fictional elements in that book. Making it into the shape of a novel, I discovered, was a matter of deciding what to leave out. Incidents that were actually spread over several years I compressed into what looked like a year and a half. I left out almost all the people who were then so busily crowding through my life. A few neighbours appeared briefly. Marguerite did not appear at all. It was written almost as if Robert and I inhabited a world of our own in a wilderness cabin, which was far, indeed, from being the case. And yet the book is true, not only technically, but in spirit.

This was a kind of nature writing that was beginning to be published in the United States at the time, but it was years ahead of its time in Canada. Here was a book that deserved public attention if any non-fiction book of mine ever did. Instead it was ignored, by the critics, the juries and the public. Canadians bought about 2,000 copies of the first edition, a few of them at marked-down prices. Fortunately, the Americans saved it—not only bought it, but named it best scientific book of the year. In 1968 the English edition came out with Peter Davies, sold very badly, and I was able to buy 1200 remaindered copies for fifty cents each. I sold all those books to bookstores in Toronto, St. John's and Annapolis Royal for prices ranging from $2 to $5 each, so that in the end I made a profit of about $3,000—more than I'd earned on the first Canadian edition. Eight years after first publication, Paperjacks took it, and it became a national best seller in the mass market. By now, too, some critics were calling it a Canadian classic, but I had mixed feelings about this. Some dreadful nature writing in a nineteenth century style was also being called "classic." Bits and pieces of *Foxes* were widely used in school books and anthologies, but only rarely treated as high-class literature—as when G. Brender à Brandis combined quotations from *Foxes* with his superb engravings to produce books of interest to collectors and art lovers.

On March 1, 1966 Farley, Claire, and John de Visser flew in by helicopter from Burgeo and landed in my garden at Beachy Cove to the utter astonishment of the neighbours, who had never seen a helicopter at close quarters before. The stunt was something of an anticlimax, because I happened to be in St. John's that day. Joey Smallwood had chartered the helicopter to bring the Mowats to St. John 's for a testimonial dinner. He was in his testimonial dinner period, holding the dinners in the dining hall of Memorial University for any world-famous figures he could capture. Eleanor Roosevelt and Rockwell Kent were among his prizes. Discovering such a distinguished writer as Farley in his midst, Joey was determined to get some use out of him. Also, he had dreams that Mowat might write his biography. Little did he suspect that it was I, formerly his worst enemy, who would eventually undertake this task. (I didn't suspect it, either, until much later.)

That was my first meeting with John de Visser, and I took the opportunity, in what short time we had together, to introduce him to some of the visual pleasures of the St. John's region—places such as Marine Drive, the little fishing hamlets near Cape St. Francis, and the Cliff Path just beyond my own back door. He promptly fell in love with coastal Newfoundland, made thousands of pictures in the island, and finally did a book with me, twenty years after his first visit.

On the evening of their arrival Marguerite joined us for drinks in the Mowats' suite at the Newfoundland Hotel. Then we repaired to Bill Pruett's place for more drinks, and finally to even more drinks at Torbay.*

Next day some of us went to the Mowat suite to drink eggnog (which Farley theorized might be less destructive than rum to the stomach) and finally we met the St. John's elite at the dinner, where we had a rip-roaring good time, which is more than you can say for most official banquets.

Farley was very diffident about venturing onto my turf, but he did it anyway. Mainland writers as a class find Newfoundland

---

* Pruett was the first taiga ecologist in Canada, had been blackballed by American universities for opposing the use of atomic explosives to dig canals, and was one of the biologists who vetted *Foxes*.

impossible to resist. If they know little about it they create a fantasy Newfoundland out of their imaginations, with a few titbits from *The Dictionary of Newfoundland English*. Farley's Newfoundland had some elements of fantasy, especially his romantic view of the noble outport pioneer, but he got a lot of it right. He was worried that I might be jealous of the fuss the government was making over him. But just then he had nothing to worry about. I was floating around on cloud nine, with *Foxes* gone to press, "one great shout of joy from cover to cover...affirmation of life, the glories of man and the universe..." as it was described. No one who has just written a book like that can be jealous of anyone else. But he was right about one thing. I do regard his Newfoundland material as somewhat flawed, and could have helped him edit it into better shape if he had asked. But that doesn't in the least detract from my admiration of him as a writer of great power and imagination.

In my time I have been helping to transform the world—not directly, by preaching in the marketplace, but by sowing seeds of future harvests among the elite. By the elite I mean the people who think, and who read selectively to stimulate thought. I never wanted to lead a crusade. Much better to leave that to people like David Suzuki and Elizabeth May who do it very successfully, even though I can't bear to listen to them myself.

And if you have spoken your "ten true words" and somehow gotten them recorded, how could you care about symbolic honours from the people who run the affairs of governments?

Farley and I also visited Joey on his ranch at Roache's Line. I suppose he assumed Farley would refuse the visit unless I was included. He appeared friendly enough, and loved showing off his treasures—his wine cellar with its secret entranceway, his collection of rare books rebound in Portuguese leather, his bronze busts. He was friendly enough to Mowat, and friendly in a cool way even to me, now that I'd forsworn political journalism for more civilized forms of writing, but nothing came of his plan to charm Farley into being his biographer. Farley not only didn't take Joey all that seriously, but also doubted his competence as biographer for a public figure. It was another twenty years before he decided to write about Dian Fossey and her attempt to save the mountain gorillas, a story that included two of his favourite themes: a doomed animal species and man's brutality toward his fellow creatures.

Chapter 5

I had many good friends among Canadian writers, none closer than Margaret Laurence, who indeed treated almost every writer she met as a member of her family. Some of them became perfect nuisances, too, but I'll not mention those. Margaret tended to be victimized not only by aspiring scribblers, but also by women, and even men, who came weeping on her shoulder when their marriages had gone down the drain. She and I were contemporaries in age and experience, and enjoyed many of the same things in addition to our writing.

She had begun her career as an international writer, lived abroad for many years, and published four books set in foreign countries before she ever tackled a Canadian theme, but eventually she became a vigorous proponent of what I call "the Canadian bibliography"—the creation of a Canadian literary culture. She took an interest in the work of every serious writer in Canada—and indeed it was in our time that a Canadian literary culture began to come into being. There had been Canadian writers before this, of course, but they had been sporadic and isolated. It was only in the 1960s and later that there began to be a literary culture in this country. Margaret and I and our colleagues of the 1960s and 1970s were in at the birth of this great cultural event, which was similar in some ways to the birth of the American literary culture a hundred years earlier (in the time of Thoreau and Emerson and Hawthorne and Poe and Melville and Whitman, all of whom were contemporaries).

The scores of Canadian writers who began publishing in the 1960s and 1970s were our personal friends. To many of them we gave encouragement and other forms of help when they needed it, sending them back to their typewriters when they were close to despair, promoting them for Canada Council grants when they were broke, demanding that governments take note of Canadian culture, even creating the concept of a "cultural industry" as a major employer, worthy of as much official attention as trucking or retail merchandising.

EEDIE STEINER

Margaret Laurence

Though she didn't actively fraternize with pop writers, Margaret wasn't hostile to them. When we were organizing the Writers' Union of Canada she said to me, "We want the people who write the Harlequin Romances and the nurse books, as well as the serious writers." The only writers she disliked were those producing the hybrid literature that falls somewhere between honest pop and true mainline fiction. Arthur Hailey might be considered a leading exponent of this genre, and she seemed to be quite angry at the extravagant success of his books. In fact, Margaret resented seeing people of small ability earn stacks of money while she and others with literary gifts received so little. She felt this way about deans of English departments and academic vice- presidents, some of whom qualified as colleagues of ours because they had published a book or two.

I first met her at d'Escousse on Cape Breton Island, where we were both visiting Silver Donald Cameron. She had returned to Canada during her long stay in England, which was still her official home at that time, and had landed in Nova Scotia with a forty-pound suitcase which she had taken on the plane as cabin luggage. She refused to be parted from it even when she stood at the lectern of Dalhousie University to deliver the convocation address and receive her honourary degree. It was the latest draft of her most ambitious novel, *The Diviners*.

"Nearly a million words of toil, sweat and tears," she told me. "Now I've got to take an axe to it and chop out all the nonsense and the fancy work. And then...well...after all that, nobody is going to publish it."

Laurence was already a legendary figure in Canadian letters, living ancestor of a gathering army of women writers, but she was a persistent pessimist about her chances with publishers and book buyers. She'd said something equally pessimistic about her novel, *The Fire Dwellers*: "Who wants to read about a middle-aged housewife, mother of four?" It turned out that a lot of middle-aged housewives did. Like Stacey in *The Fire Dwellers*, and Alice's Red Queen, they were running as fast as they could just to stay in the same place.

Margaret was already at the peak of her career before she realized that her readers, like Winnie the Pooh, wanted to hear stories about themselves, and that she was just the writer to tell them such stories because she, too, was a middle-aged, middle-class housewife, struggling to make ends meet without enough cups for the instant coffee, worrying that her kids were running around with a crowd of pot-smokers, still recovering from a failed marriage.

Unlike most creative writers of her time, Margaret would never even touch a "reefer." The mere smell of a burning joint scared her. But she consumed whiskey and tobacco without stint. There was always a burning cigarette, but never a glass of booze, next to her typewriter. Weekend binges were a regular part of her life, and she could "hold her liquor" with the most hardened drinkers. I saw her put away forty ounces of twelve-year-old Scotch between four P.M. and midnight, then get up for church the next morning without a sign of a hangover.

Because she expressed so perfectly the frustrations that so many women in North America experienced, the feminists rushed to take her into their camp, but they got a cool reception (as they did also from Margaret Atwood and Marian Engel and Alice Munro). "I'm all for women's lib," she said, "but I'm not for women attacking men. Men aren't the enemy. They need to be liberated, too."

Peggy Wemyss, as they still called her in her home town of Neepawa, Manitoba, was central Canadian in every sense: born in mid-country, middle-class to the core, from a family of merchants and lawyers, of Irish-Scottish ancestry. Her friends always included neighbourhood shopkeepers and dressmakers. To everyone in the towns where she lived she was a neighbouring housewife, carrying her plastic shopping bag from the supermarket. The image didn't change, even when she was famous, even after she had received every honour her own country could bestow, and was on the short list for a Nobel Prize.

Her childhood was filled with death that cast a shadow over all her work. Her mother died when she was four, and her father married his sister-in-law, but he died too five years later. Among other deaths in her childhood were a grandmother and a boy next door.

"My stepmother, my Aunt Margaret, was a kind, wonderful woman who always seemed to be my real mother," she said. "A teacher and librarian, she had a great feeling for literature, and her house was full of books. But she didn't have such influence on me as that terrible old man."

The terrible old man was her maternal grandfather, undertaker for the town of Neepawa. After her father died, Peggy and her aunt moved into the old man's house, and the eighty-year-old patriarch, grim and demanding, became an ever-present spectre until she escaped to college in Winnipeg at the age of seventeen.

Did he beat her?

"Yes, though not often."

The passage in *The Stone Angel* which describes the boys getting whipped with birch rods "because they were boys, and older," but the girl not entirely escaping either, is clearly autobiographical. "I hated him, but I'm sure he stiffened me for life. If I'm a fighter, he made me one. It was a constant battle of wills with Grandfather John Simpson: no parties, no dances, no boyfriends." She was the only member of the family who would stand up to him. Her knees buckled; she had to hold something to keep from trembling, but she stood up. The death of her kindly maternal grandmother happened when she was eleven.

Margaret was never beautiful in any conventional sense. Even as a small child she had the heavy face and wide mouth that she abhorred as an adult. But her face was full of compassion and kindness; she never realized how this illuminated her rather coarse features. Numerous photographs survive—from childhood and later. The worst of them, in my opinion, is that ridiculous, untruthful picture chosen for the dust jacket of James King's biography. This photograph, in which Margaret looks like the Queen of Egypt, offended me so deeply that I removed the damned thing when I read the book. She liked this ridiculous picture herself, but that just shows how wrong we are likely to be when judging ourselves or presenting a public image. Unfortunate if this should become the Margaret Laurence image in the Canadian mind, because Margaret was diametrically opposite to the vain, aloof film star here portrayed. She was much more the typical housewife, worried about money, worried about her health but continuing her unhealthy habits, worried about her adult children, divorced but heterosexually active, taking part in every good cause from the fire department's bake sales to the national peace movement, going to church faithfully Sunday mornings, with tastes in art and music that never went beyond calendar pictures and the hymn book. Indeed, though she had been subjected to music lessons as a child, she had no musical sense at all. She professed fondness for bagpipes, but I always thought this was part of her pose as a "black Celt." The only way she was extraordinary was in her literary sense, which encompassed the whole field of writing—that, and perhaps her character, her ability to work so hard and so well at the difficult craft of mainline fiction.

She was very ambitious for success, her whole life directed into her career. She even worried about the eventual survival of her work, and once said to me, in a tone of regret, "You know, Harold, if any of us are read in the next century, it's likely to be Graham Greene." This suggests the conservative cast of her tastes, and of her own writing. She didn't expect any of the young Turks to last very long, but rather the most mainstream of contemporary novelists, the successors to Conrad.

But Margaret and I didn't have a *professional* relationship. We weren't furthering each other's careers. She didn't need my help, and I certainly wasn't looking for hers, so we had a kind of friendship different from that which she enjoyed with so many other writers. This should be evident even from what survives of our correspondence. We weren't discussing literary problems, the subtleties of "voice" and so on (a great concern among writers just then) or any of the other matters discussed in her voluminous correspondence with the Can-lit circle. We were having fun, enjoying each other's company even when we were living in places as distant as Beachy Cove and the Otonobee River. We hardly discussed our own writing, though she was fully aware of what was going on even out on the edge, where I was writing what was then regarded as "experimental" fiction while she remained committed to conservative structures that hadn't ventured beyond Doris Lessing. Her understanding of the new literature, of the radical voice, of the world beyond Faulkner was illustrated by her championing of *The New Ancestors*, that remarkable novel by Dave Godfrey, which never succeeded in the traditional sense because it was too structurally complex for North American readers.*

"As a teenager, my great dread was that I'd be trapped in Neepawa for the rest of my life," she recalled. "No way was my grandfather going to send me to college. He didn't believe in educating women, so I worked like a dog for a scholarship, got it, and went off to the church-sponsored United College in Winnipeg." There she not only encountered professors who gave her a good grounding in English literature, but also became familiar with the King James translation of the Bible, which shaped her style and outlook for life (as it did with me, and many other writers of our generation).

In college they thought of her as a rebel. Her heroes were Dr. Norman Bethune, who had died for the Communist revolution in China, and Louis Riel, who had led the Northwest Rebellion, and was hanged by the Canadian government. This won her few friends in college, but got her noticed by the radical press, and landed her a job on the socialist *Winnipeg Citizen*.

"That makes me a certified member of the Old Left," she announced proudly thirty years later. By then the New Left had become trendy with a new generation of students who never had

---

* A curious thing happened with this book. Either Godfrey or his Canadian publisher (New Press) must have submitted it to Doubleday in New York, hoping for American publication. Doubleday wrote a respectful letter of rejection explaining why they couldn't take a chance on such a book, and mailed the letter to me by mistake.

the good fortune to encounter the King James Bible. "Working for a newspaper was a great experience. Meeting daily and weekly deadlines is just the kind of discipline that every writer needs, and it makes you really at home with a typewriter. You also get to meet all kinds of people, many of them in great stress and tragedy. Perfect training for a fiction writer...only..." She paused to give a rueful smile, "it's impossible to do both things together. When you write journalism all day, you're too exhausted to write fiction, and you need the weekend just to recover." In Winnipeg she met Adele Wiseman, with whom she formed a lifelong friendship. In later years Adele became an unfortunate influence—a disappointed and embittered writer who encouraged Margaret to abandon the Writers' Union and try to tear it apart at its most critical period—an action that left Margaret psychologically damaged for the rest of her life.

Margaret is sometimes described as the first Chair of the Writers' Union of Canada, and credited with a great deal of work in organizing it. She is described as "a driving force in the organization" throughout its early history. This is hardly correct. Margaret never accepted the Chair. She was interim Chair for ten months in 1973, before the union was organized, before it held its founding convention, but this was essentially an honourary position. She was "lending her name" to the organization, while the work of organizing fell to such people as Graeme Gibson, Marian Engel, Margaret Atwood, Rudy Wiebe, and myself.

Marian Engel was the union's first Chair. Rudy Wiebe and I were Vice-Chairs. During the first year we held weekly meetings by conference phone. Marian began immediately campaigning for Public Lending Right, a campaign that succeeded after twelve years of lobbying, and put three million dollars a year into the pockets of Canadian writers. Meanwhile, I drafted and piloted the by-laws, and later wrote a book of rules for the union and the Periodical Writers' Association—a job I had done previously for various trade unions and other volunteer organizations. I continued as Vice-Chair the second year, when Graeme Gibson became Chair.

It was also in Winnipeg that Margaret met her husband Jack Laurence, and sailed with him to London, almost penniless, beginning her prolonged if intermittent exile from Canada. There she landed a job with an employment agency, and he with an engineering firm. Within a year he had what he wanted—a government posting to build dams in the Somali desert.

Margaret plunged straight into African life, got an interpreter to help her with the language, and within two years had the first collection of Somali literature ever committed to writing. Published in 1954, her first book, *A Tree for Poverty*, made such a cultural impact on the country that the Somalis invited her back, eleven years later, to be part of their independence celebrations. From Somalia came a second book, *The Prophet's Camel Bell*.

The Laurences were next posted to Ghana, a country in a state of chaos, plunging toward independence with enormous excitement, which Margaret caught successfully in her first novel, *This Side Jordan*. From Ghana came, also, her first book of short stories, *The Tomorrow-Tamer*. During her seven years in Africa her two children were born.

The family then spent four years in Vancouver, where Jack Laurence had yet another engineering job, and a full social life in what was for Margaret a dull and boring circle of engineers and middle-class social climbers.

"After the African nationalists and poets and drummers, it was like being tossed into a swamp," she told me. "Surely life wasn't meant to be so dull, so utterly boring!" This was the part of her career she cared least to discuss, but she turned it into fiction, just the same, when she wrote *The Fire Dwellers*.

Her marriage had now begun to break down. Margaret was unsuited to accompanying an engineer around the world as part of his baggage, and she refused to follow Jack to India, his next posting. Meanwhile her English publisher had found a rental cottage halfway between London and Oxford where she could try being full-time writer and full-time mother.

Out of Elm Cottage came her first Canadian book, a blockbuster that many readers still regard as Canada's finest novel, *The Stone Angel*. In it Laurence went back to her prairie childhood and her pioneering ancestors, accomplishing the astonishing feat of writing convincingly from the point of view of a ninety-year-old woman. It was the first of the five books on which her reputation rests, all of them centering around the fictional town of Manawaka, a recreation of Neepawa, which she had never seen since the age of seventeen. When she published it, she was thirty-eight. It had taken her twenty years to find her native voice.

Canadians visiting Elm Cottage were shocked at Margaret's poverty. She smoked the cheapest "gaspers," served macaroni casserole for lunch, had a miserable little electric heater to keep the room from freezing. But there she finished her next novel, *A Jest of God*, and was deliriously happy about it.

She and I sometimes discussed the art of fiction. Her views were very conventional—straight from college English, I felt—repetitions of the stuff you heard from the academics: the depths of the human soul, the profundities that the novelist is said to explore in fiction, so much more profound than anything reached by social scientists or non-fiction writers—this I regarded as a convenient myth, propagated by novelists and critics. It's a pretense that novels are something much more important than mere entertainment: the novelist is "the bard that present, past and future sees," the "Druid gray, wood-natured, quiet-eyed," as Yeats expressed it. It's all nonsense, in my view, all incense and bells and incantation, hiding the fact that there's nothing behind it, nothing more than some play-acting around a well-worn formula, depending on the skill with which the writer can interweave the lives of characters, and make them live. Margaret fell for this stuff eventually. Hence her pretentious title, *The Diviners*. Graham Greene, who turned from the depths of the soul to the intricacies of spy fiction, was perhaps trying to be honest.

She was deeply impressed by the first volume of Robertson Davies' dive into mainline fiction, *Fifth Business*.

"It's about the *problem of evil*," she said in a hushed voice.

"So? Does it solve the problem?"

"Well...no. It explores it."

I didn't argue the point, but I later wrote about the problem of evil in *Dancing on the Shore*. In my view it's purely a social question, having nothing to do with the workings of the universe.

The teachers, and even the schoolchildren, in *A Jest of God* are so vividly drawn that I thought Margaret must have been a teacher at one time, and asked her about it.

"Oh no," she said. "I've never been a teacher. Those are people I remember from my childhood at the age of nine." Then, after a pause, she added, "I've got a novelist's memory."

Hollywood bought rights to *A Jest of God*, and changed its title to *Rachel, Rachel*. The book also won the Governor General's Award, which should, of course, have gone to *The Stone Angel* two years earlier, but the jury, as often happens, had failed to appreciate great writing when it was under their noses. (I should know about Canada Council juries. I've served on five of them.)

The film for the first time introduced Margaret to a broad popular audience in the company of famous stars, Joanne Woodward and Paul Newman, for whom it won the New York

Critics' Award. Suddenly, the shy girl from Neepawa was a celebrity. More important, from her point of view, she got $17,000 for the film rights, and with it bought Elm Cottage. It was the first time she'd had enough money to buy anything. The only other occasion when she could see beyond next month's bills was when she got the Molson Prize, more than a decade later.

"I think I'll take the Molson money and buy a piece of land," she told me, "something to leave my kids."

Elm Cottage was a place of pilgrimage for Canadians in England. Her visitors included Silver Donald Cameron, Marjorie Whitelaw, and the Newfoundland novelist Percy Janes. She was also popular with London's African community, especially with the emerging Nigerian literary movement, then taking London by storm, and she wrote a book, *Long Drums and Cannons*, on Nigerian literature.

It was then, too, that she had her great *affaire de coeur* with the Nigerian ambassador. She'd had an earlier liaison with a black writer from the West Indies, George Lamming, but her relationship with the princely African was the one she liked to remember. Silver Donald Cameron, then living in England, sometimes acted as the ambassador's ambassador, arranging their meetings. Though Margaret made no secret of the relationship, it is never mentioned in comments on Can-lit. Like her drinking, and like L.M. Montgomery's suicide, the subject was long treated as taboo in Canada. She was proud of her relations with the seven-foot black prince, and delighted with the ceremony and the *élan*. Visiting London theatres and exclusive restaurants in his chauffeur-driven Rolls-Royce was truly a world away from her horse-and-buggy days in Neepawa.

The Nigerian renaissance sank into a blood bath in 1969, and most of the intellectuals were massacred. Margaret was invited, that year, to a residency at the University of Toronto. There she discovered that she preferred Canada to England. She kept Elm Cottage for another two years, left her son and daughter there, and went there in the winter, but now did most of her writing in a cabin on the Otonobee River, near Peterborough, Ontario. I was spending my own summers in the Mowat cabin on the shore of Lake Ontario, an hour's drive away. Margaret and I worked alone throughout the week, spent weekends together, at one place or the other, and sometimes had visits from her next-door neighbour, the short story writer and former bank robber, Don Bailey, who would eventually become one of her biographers.

I pulled out the great patch of poison ivy that grew beside her door (I'm immune to its poison), ate a few of the vile-tasting berries of bittersweet nightshade, to demonstrate that it is not "deadly nightshade" as most Upper Canadians suppose, took her rowing in her punt, the *CC Grant* (named for the Canada Council grant that had paid for it) and tried unsuccessfully to teach her to prefer wine to Scotch. (She did drink wine at meals, but it never took the place of her serious drinking, which was sometimes gin and tonic, but usually whiskey.)

She always resisted her friends' attempts to make her adopt a healthier lifestyle. Helda Buck, my close friend from Toronto, tried without success to make Margaret take up vitamin supplements, which might have helped to detoxify both the alcohol and the tobacco, but she made only a half-hearted gesture in that direction. She did limit her drinking to leisure time, but that was as far as she would go. "I can't help it," she'd say, "if I'm built like a Russian peasant, and have the same kind of tastes." Her cooking was a standing joke that we tried to avoid. When she visited my family at Beachy Cove, Newfoundland (her only trip to the Rock) one of her great delights was the food in a house where three excellent cooks competed for the privilege of making dinner. "A feast every day!" she exulted.

Food aside, the Otonobee was a good place for a writer—miles from the nearest highroad, approached by a confusing tangle of country lanes. Nobody got there without a map. Her desk overlooked the water, neighbours stayed out of her way except to bring her gifts of freshwater fish; writers, editors and publishers were all warned to stay away from Monday morning until Friday noon.

She loved the Ontario countryside. Swallows built nests above her window, and she eagerly watched the young birds learn to fly. She prowled about the grounds barefoot (after the poison ivy was gone) and sat on the little dock jotting notes with a pencil, but most of the time she was lost in the private world of her fiction. It took all Monday morning to "get inside the story" where she'd stay until Friday noon, now and then snacking absent-mindedly on a sandwich or splurging on a bowl of cauliflower soup. Then she'd come down out of it, slightly dazed, and be ready for a non-stop weekend party.

I asked about the title of her new book, but she wouldn't mention it: "I have a wonderful title, but I'm superstitious about discussing it before publication. And I don't discuss drafts, either. But the title will be first-rate, like *The Stone Angel* and *A Jest of God*. I've got a real gift for names. I renamed some of the places where I grew up. Clear Lake became Diamond Lake—think how much better that is! Galloping Mountain is a great improvement over Riding Mountain. You were lucky in Newfoundland. If only we'd had a few retired pirates on the prairies, we might have had names like Seldom-Come-By and Black Joke Cove."

Though she wouldn't show her own drafts, she read many manuscripts by other writers, and recommended them for grants. She recommended me on the only occasion when I applied for a major arts grant for fiction, and she recommended Des Walsh while he was still an unknown young poet with his first slim volume in print. He had never met her, but when he got the grant he went to visit her, bearing a bottle of twelve-year-old Scotch.

"You'll be able to tell your grandchildren that you knew Margaret Laurence," I said. Her support helped Walsh to become one of Newfoundland's first full-time writers.

Though we didn't discuss our writing, she admired some of the things I was doing: "*The Foxes of Beachy Cove* hasn't just influenced me," she said. "It changed my life. I can't say that about any other book since *Tropic of Cancer*."

When she read a draft of *Remembering Summer* she was deeply impressed: "That just knocks me over. I really envy you. I really do. Here you are at middle age, same as me, and you're able to launch out into this wonderful piece of experimental fiction. All 1 can do is the same kind of thing I was doing twenty years ago."

"So what should I do with it? Take it to a small press?"

"*No!*" She was emphatic. "Take it to one of the big publishers, and *make* them publish it. That's where we belong, at McClelland and Stewart or Macmillan or Doubleday."

Marian Engel had the same advice: "Stick with your biggest publisher. Maybe they'll lose money on one of your books. So what? They owe it to you."

Despite this, I took *Remembering Summer* back from Doubleday, who had grudgingly agreed to publish it, knowing it would never earn them a dime, did a thorough final revision on the computer at the University of Waterloo, and sent it to Pottersfield Press, who not only published it, but did a second release at the same time they published my fourth novel, *Evening Light*, in 1997. I have rarely regretted taking some of my work to small presses. They have a vital place in Canadian culture, and deserve to get some of the best writing being done.

I've published with the four biggest publishers in Canada, but some of my best work has been published in small editions by such presses as Pottersfield in Nova Scotia and Killick in Newfoundland. For me they have always done beautiful work, producing books that are a joy to see and handle. A beautiful book can be as important to me as a big sale.

After a long gestation *The Diviners* appeared in 1974. No book in Canada had ever enjoyed such a reception. Critics praised it. Margaret got her second Governor General's Award, the Order of Canada, and the Molson Prize. Trent University made her its chancellor. When she rose to speak at the annual banquet of the Writers' Union of Canada (which she still supported at that time, and whose members she regarded as "her tribe") she was still shaking with stage fright, and had to hold herself up by the back of a chair, but her fellow writers gave her an ovation. Even Neepawa invited her home for civic honours.

But there were contrary opinions. One old neighbour, facing the camera of the National Film Board, stated angrily, "I never thought little Peggy Wemyss would write such...such ...*stuff.*"

The objection was to the street language in some of the oral stories some of her characters told, but there was another objection, even stronger, never stated publicly. In *The Diviners* a respectable white woman, a professor's wife, is having an affair with the Canadian equivalent of a nigger—a Métis folk singer, "half-breed Indian" as they were called. School board members who hadn't opened a book since their own school days went around telling each other that they weren't going to have their teenaged daughters reading the likes of *that*. The book was banned, unread, in Peterborough.

"I have finished the work that was given me to do," she said, echoing one of her favourite writers, St. Paul. "Yet there might still be something required of me." Personally, I found this pretense that she had a mission from God rather annoying. I do not regard mainline fiction as the modern equivalent of the Epistles to the Corinthians.

She turned to battling censorship and social injustice. But she did even this out of a sense of desperation. She believed that the gift had been withdrawn. After 1974 she wrote some children's stories, collected her journalism into a book, and made a number of starts on novels, none of which succeeded. One of the themes she tried unsuccessfully and dropped was later developed by Margaret Atwood into *The Handmaid's Tale*, which became one of the most successful Canadian novels after *The Diviners*. I don't believe Atwood picked up the theme from Laurence. It was simply there, demanding the attention of a serious writer.

Despite disagreement over Writers' Union policy, Margaret and I remained friends for the rest of her life. She had always acted as if nothing could touch her. Besides being a lifelong chain-smoker, she worked too hard, got no physical exercise, ignored all the rules of nutrition, and loved to sit with friends drinking through most of the night. In the last twelve years of her life she developed diabetes (fortunately not severe), then cataracts that threatened blindness until cured by surgery, and finally lung cancer. As happened with several other friends of mine who were killed by tobacco, the cancer was discovered too late for surgery to correct it.

One of the last times I spoke with her, by phone shortly before her death, she broke out into the chesty chuckles that we all knew so well: "Oh wow! I've made it to the age of sixty! How lucky I am!" By now she could feel death approaching, knew that she had inoperable cancer, but expressed no self-pity except in the privacy of her diary.

Some years earlier she had said, "Most of the disasters that other people experience eventually overtake you, too." She was prepared for such disasters as blindness, acute disability, even the loss of mental powers, and had begun to write notes for her memoirs. Now she worked at the job seriously. Before Christmas 1986, when she was still feeling strong, she slipped on the ice and broke an ankle, spending the next few weeks in bed. Unable to work at her desk or use a typewriter, she continued work on her memoirs by dictation. She finished the book, except, perhaps for a final revision, and it was published posthumously.

The very last time I spoke with her, just before she died, she used exactly the same words as Alden Nowlan, the last time I spoke with him: "Keep the faith, Harold," she said.

She died of metastacized lung cancer (death hastened slightly by a self-administered overdose of sedatives) on January 4, 1987. A thousand mourners crowded Bloor Street United Church in Toronto for a memorial service, and sang the familiar hymn "Old Hundred:"

> All people that on earth do dwell
> Sing to the Lord with joyful voice.
> Him serve with mirth, His praise forthtell;
> Come ye before Him and rejoice!

Hardly a funeral dirge. Margaret, who had written the service herself, chose it for that very reason. She did not regard her death as a tragedy, but almost as a fulfilment, like the period at the end of a well-written book.

They played the bagpipes over her, too, for she had become one of the ancestors.

Chapter 6

I lived at Beachy Cove (with breaks in Ontario) for seventeen years, from the summer of 1961 until the early spring of 1979, the longest period I ever lived in one place until I moved to Upper Clements on the Annapolis Basin. It was a period of great personal change and social upheaval. I arrived a freelance journalist, trying to escape from the miseries of civilization. I departed after having scored notable successes with several books, while remaining personally anonymous. Canada must be one of the few countries in the world where you can write a string of national best sellers without becoming personally known to the reading public. It is media attention, especially on television, not the authorship of books, that makes Canadian writers famous. The media attention may have nothing at all to do with writing—indeed, usually does not. The projection of an intriguing image is the route to fame. Millions of viewers will instantly recognize Mowat or Atwood on TV. Not one in a hundred of those viewers will ever buy one of their books.

Fortunately for me, I had little media attention. I saw others become media stars, as well as successful writers, and shrank from what they had to do. The kind of constant public attention they received would have killed me. In a good year I could sell fifty thousand or even a hundred thousand books (mostly paperbacks) without being famous, and that, for me, was much the better way. I hankered for a private life as well as for success in the market, and discovered that it is possible, though difficult, to have both.

Life at Beachy Cove was romantic and pleasant, with wild little beaches below the cliffs, a river pool deep enough for high dives, a small lake, a trout stream and trout gully, all within easy walking distance. *The Foxes of Beachy Cove* and *Remembering Summer* tell something about life there, mainly at the beginning and end of the sixties when humanity was "going off like a bomb," as I expressed it, and Beachy Cove became one of the Meccas for dropouts from all parts of North America.

Children of all ages, including those at the edge of adulthood, have always flocked to me unasked. This, together with my ingrained radicalism and my tolerance for the unconventional, made me one of the gurus of the sixties. In a sense I was already a hippie before the first hippie was hatched, already fond of music, birds, flowers, and even butterflies, already wearing beard and sandals and flowing locks, already loving scores of people, instead of only the woman who shared my bed.

Children not yet in their teens came to me because I loved them (a thing rarer than you might suppose among North Americans) and because I treated them as friends and equals, not merely as pets. During my years as a journalist I was attacked for this as well as for supposed communism, and for consorting with female prostitutes. The attack on my private life, which in fact was decent and discreet, was based on nothing more than a journalist's interest in all classes of people. In fact, I consorted with hard-core criminals oftener than with prostitutes, but the politicians seem to have missed this. I took the kids fishing and camping and canoeing. Some were the sons and daughters of friends and neighbours; others I met by accident; some came to me for free tutoring with school work. With a few of them I developed an intensely emotional relationship, but my behaviour was above reproach by any standards: never, at any time, did I seek sexual pleasure with a boy or girl. During the "liberation" of the sixties, teenagers, both boys and girls, sometimes made sexual advances to me. I rejected them, gently but firmly.

Our relationships were mutually enriching. The boy to whom I was closest in the fifties, Charles Richardson, later achieved considerable success in business, as well as socially, rising many steps above the status of his family. I take credit for helping him toward his maturity. I was master of ceremonies at his wedding, godfather to his eldest child.

In the fifties a smear based on the suspicion of homosexuality, without a shred of evidence, could be as disastrous as a charge of communism. It is hard for us to credit now how serious such character assassination could be. You could be fired, blacklisted, ostracised and if unlucky sent to jail for the one or for the other. The risk of being framed for political reasons on a sex charge—a risk I ran continuously from 1953 to 1961—was one of the origins of the plot of *Tomorrow Will Be Sunday*. But, apart from the hassle of being followed around by plainclothes policemen, nothing came of it.

There was the added danger that the kids themselves could be harmed by people aiming to harm me. This presented the sort of dilemma that might tempt you either to withdraw from the public lists, seeking a safer occupation than political journalism, or to withdraw from the company of the children, depriving yourself of emotional and spiritual pleasure, and depriving the children of the lifelong enrichment that (you hoped) the relationship might provide.

In the end, I accepted neither of those options, but walked boldly and cautiously along the street called straight, attempting to fulfill my self-appointed missions in public and private. When I did finally withdraw from the political lists it was not because I had been bribed, intimidated, or driven from the field, but because my own effectiveness as a political journalist was waning, and because, like Thoreau, I had "other lives to live."

The love of someone outside the family can be of immense value to a child. The sense of self-worth that it engenders, the sense of reassurance and security, the sense of solidarity with a wider human community can undoubtedly alter the course of a child's life for the better and even hasten in a small measure "that one far-off divine event toward which the whole creation moves."

Love takes many forms, and various people have varying capacities. Thoreau, loving ten-year-old Edmund Sewall so profoundly that he felt compelled to express his love in a noble and anguished and somewhat pathetic lyric, could not by his nature open his arms to the boy at first meeting and say, "Come." He was held at a distance by "stern respect," and it was only after Edmund's parents had read the poem and had taken the initiative of thrusting the young philosopher and the boy together that Thoreau and Edmund became intimate as student and tutor.

Thoreau was clearly right about the need for respect. Without it, love can be selfish and exploitive. The laird who "possessed" the maid on the kitchen table, the master of horse who buggered the boy in the barn, were not expressing love at all but a vicious possessiveness that is the very essence of rape. And this essence remains the same inside or outside marriage, in hetero- and homosexual relationships. We speak correctly when we refer to the rape of the environment by corporations, or of the land by mechanized farming.

It is typical of our culture that exploitation is presupposed. Paedophilia, regarded by Greek philosophers as a noble form of love, has become, among us, a pseudonym for buggery. Love between adults and children is, in our society, always suspect, so that even teachers are afraid to express openly their love for their students. The result is to raise the kind of barrier that Thoreau agonized over, to increase the frigidity of society and to impoverish the emotional lives of those groping toward adulthood.

Emotionally deprived children who have received nothing more than mothering (and often not even that) are expected to blossom instantly with the help of illustrated glosses on the Kama Sutra, into responsive adults capable of mature and unselfish relationships. No wonder so many of them remain emotionally frigid for life. No wonder so many of their marriages end in divorce. No wonder they confuse love with exploitation. What else could be expected from people raised in a society whose attitudes toward love and loving are so utterly barbaric.

Because of such convictions, because children followed me to Beachy Cove from the city, adding to those from the neighbourhood, and because adult friends with or without literary ambitions also flocked around me, regarding my place as an open house, there was no way, once the sixties came to flower, that I could escape being the centre of The Scene, as it was called, for the province of Newfoundland.

I saw my first acid trip at Christmas—a mild enough affair it was, to all appearances—and had visits from a handful of students throughout the winter. And then, one sunny evening in June, I returned from the city to find fifteen teenagers in my sitting room playing The Fugs and The Doors on my record player. Most of them I had never seen before, but one young man who had been in and out of my house for several months was reassuring: "Just wait," he said, "this is only the beginning."

Soon there were tents permanently erected in my back field, and a tarpaulin that had once been a cover for a transport truck converted into a kind of community centre. The inhabitants of the tents kept walking through the house. If you included the daybed in the kitchen and the pull-out davenport in the sitting room, there was sleeping accomodation for eight or nine people in the house, but soon they were sleeping in the overstuffed chairs, and then on the floor. An old Persian rug in front of an open fire is not such a bad place to sleep. I tried it myself on nights when my bed was preempted by mated couples. Occasionally I found myself alone for an hour or two, but usually I was surrounded by young people, often from a dozen different places in Canada and the United States, on pilgrimage to Beachy Cove, directed there by the underground telegraph. Very soon it was no longer an easy place to immerse yourself in the difficult job of creative writing—or any kind of writing, for that matter.

I loved it, in spite of the pandemonium, and perhaps that was why I managed to accomplish so much. *One Door Into Darkness* was hardly out of the way before I was deep into another novel in addition to *Remembering Summer*. Indeed, I went to Doubleday and signed a two-novel contract, and took an advance. One of those novels was to be *Remembering Summer*, and the other "a novel set in Labrador." I didn't realize then that *Remembering Summer* wouldn't be finished until 1986.

White Eskimo, the Labrador novel, gave me no trouble at all. I didn't write it straight through. I began by writing a piece about Gillingham's arrival in Nain. Then I wrote a chapter on a fight with a white bear, much as if it were a short story. I wrote a sketch of Gillingham's adopted daughter, Halfbreed, again as if I were doing a short story. At some point I decided to have the story told by two narrators at an all-night party in the lounge of the coastal ship *Kyle* as she headed northward along the coast of Labrador. So I went back to the beginning, and started to write a connected narrative.

While this was going on I was acting as friend and protector to bearded giants aged sixteen to eighteen from Gander and

Corner Brook and St. John's, and to young men and women from Georgia and Alaska and British Columbia and points between, some of them poets, some of them drug freaks, some of them quite capable of stealing cars or looting deserted houses. I put up bail for them when they needed it, and some people misinterpreted this as approval of what they were doing. Far from it. In the case of one young American who had been deported to the United States after I'd helped him with bail and a lawyer, I learned that he was planning to sneak back into Canada, and I warned the authorities to keep an eye out for him. Once or twice parents phoned me in states of murderous fury because I'd put up bail for their son or daughter whom they wanted to see punished by imprisonment without trial. No use to explain that bail was everyone's civil right. That just drove them to even greater fury. In their world, people under the age of twenty-five *had* no civil rights.

I do not need to record all that happened in the era of the flower children and the greasers because the essence, the spirit of it all, is recorded in *Remembering Summer*. Many things are left out of the novel, of course, just because it is a novel, not an autobiography.

Somewhere in this period I met Leslie McGrath walking along Duckworth Street, and found myself with another person who was to change my life. Leslie was a wild child, one of the younger members of the extensive family of talented children of Dr. Jim and Anita McGrath. Jim had been a friend of mine when he was Deputy Minister of Health, and later when he was a minister in Smallwood's government. Leslie had remained wild after her marriage to Miller Ayre, chief scion of a clan of millionaire merchants. She remained wild after the birth of her two children. The marriage had broken down by the time I met her, and Leslie was busy with "the revolution," which she viewed not as a political event, but one of personal liberation for each individual.

Among her numerous projects—she was forever starting things, then leaving them to others—was a free school in St. John's, an alternative for high-school students who were dropping out (or, far more often, being *kicked* out) of the public schools run by the denominational school boards. It was a time when you could be expelled from school for wearing your hair longer than the vice-principal thought proper, for wearing a white silk shirt (Robert's sin, that got him thrown out of Prince of Wales) or for coming to school in sandals instead of "proper" shoes—any symbol of nonconformity, in fact.

Animal Farm was one of three experimental schools started at St. John's in the late summer of 1969. The other two accomodated small children, and were organized by parents who thought their children were being cheated by the school system. Animal Farm was intended for young adults, for those who had finished high-school, or had dropped out of the late grades, or needed help and encouragement, a place to relax and work while trying to finish school within the existing system. Almost fifty percent of our students were registered at other schools, which continued to receive government grants on their behalf while giving them nothing in return, not even a seat or a desk.

Some of those who were and some of those who were not registered at other schools completed a full academic year at Animal Farm, and wrote and passed the public exams for grade ten or eleven. A few others attended regularly to work beyond the high-school level, reading such subjects as astronomy, sociology and anthropology. A lot of English literature beyond high-school was read there too. One student who had already been accepted for the university semester beginning in the autumn of 1970 attended to do review work equivalent to the university's "foundation year" which was something like grade twelve.

Though at the beginning everyone at the school was doing some kind of academic work, there was a gradual infiltration of young people who were interested only in music and the social aspects of the school. It was a place to meet your friends, to play records, to pick out a tune on a guitar, or to find a sympathetic hearing when you were in trouble. Since many of the students were already alienated, living with hostile parents, or even, in two or three instances, homeless, it was also, in a sense, a refuge.

The two functions the school eventually served—education and a drop-in centre—did not mix well, and one or the other was always trying to swallow up its rival. The school's main problems, however, came not from such internal tensions, but from the outside, from a campaign of slander, lies and vituperation such as I would never have believed possible if I hadn't experienced it. Almost from the day it opened there was a fanatical attempt to close it, all stemming from a few people who got a furious mad-on every time they saw a boy with long hair or a girl in a maxi-skirt. This sheer, irrational, murderous hatred of young people whose only crime was that of being young and mildly different from the mass of those in their age group was the ugliest manifestation of human psychology that I have ever encountered.

My job, which at the beginning had been merely providing some of the funds, became mainly that of shield and defender—dealing with the authorities, keeping the lynch mob at arm's length, and persuading the students that keeping the school alive was more important than the grand gesture of taking to the barricades.

I'd become associated with Animal Farm very casually when Leslie invited me to attend a meeting of parents and teachers who were trying to organize a free school for their children—one where they'd be exposed to art and music and creative learning. Soon I was deep in a discussion of ways and means. Within a day or two I was attending another meeting where teachers, high-school students, and high-school graduates were discussing the possibility of a free high school.

Except for a shortage of money, they felt they were ready to begin. I felt they were not, and said so. They insisted that they could manage without full-time teachers (Leslie herself had a teaching license; so did one or two others) with little or no equipment, with only a few books. All they needed was a place, or rent money. If they could find as much as $100 a month....

On the impulse of the moment, an impulse I never regretted, I gave up my plans for a new car, and offered them the rent money. I might have hesitated had I realized what I was letting myself in for. Fortunately I did not forsee that I would have to give up not only my new car, but also the savings I was accumulating for a world trip, and any leisure time that I had hoped to enjoy.

At the end of the year I was still far from the end of my resources. It was one of my most productive periods, with royalties and advances arriving regularly. The people who tried to get me fired from *The Evening Telegram*, where I was again working part-time, hoping thereby to cut off the school's finances, underestimated me as well as *The Telegram*. The Herders, who owned and ran the paper, wouldn't be bullied by a loud-mouthed faction of the public any more than by the government, which had tried it earlier and failed. I didn't bear the financial burden alone. Some parents supported the school generously. Some educators made valuable gifts. We had thousands of dollars worth of excellent books, all but a handful of them donated. The students too contributed, but their means were very slender. Some had literally nothing. Two boys whose parents refused to pay the registration fee for the public examinations went out on the street and panhandled the money themselves. They both graduated.

In theory, we charged the students a dollar a month. They paid it if they could. But essentially it was a free school not only in the sense that it was run by students rather than a committee of adults, but also in the sense that you didn't have to pay fees. To help with expenses, some of Leslie's friends chipped in, including a youth group that ran a weekly TV show, and so had a bit of cash. I traded my last insurance policy (which had been intended to help with Robert's education) and put the money into the school. Civil servants in the Department of Education supplied us with textbooks sent to them by publishers looking for orders. So did one of the professors at the university. Almost overnight we acquired an impressive library dealing with both the hard and soft sciences. I loaned reference books, including a set of the Encyclopaedia Britannica. I also set up a darkroom with an excellent enlarger and other equipment that had been in storage since I had moved from Campbell Avenue. The students played around with photography but produced nothing very original. Much more interesting was the collection of posters and graffiti that appeared on the walls, everything from images of Che Guevara to the "Fly United" poster showing birds copulating in flight.

All teaching was by volunteers. A gentleman named Fred Scott, who worked for CBC and loved the French language, taught classes in French. A student teacher at Memorial gave regular lectures in history. Another ran a program of audio-visual education, using films from the university's collection, and from the National Film Board. One of the most popular was an ancient anti-drug film named *Reefer Madness* which everyone regarded as absolutely hilarious. I tutored people in math and physics, and ran a very popular class in grade eleven math. Don Walsh, a student doing grade eleven math, and no other subject, taught algebra, geometry and number theory to the youngest members of the school. In my math classes we did all the work as round-table problem solving, working in groups of twos and threes. It was a new experience for the students to encounter a teacher who had a profound understanding of mathematics, and an appreciation of the aesthetics of the subject. Some of them would skip film if it conflicted with the math class. It was almost the only practical use I ever found for one of my favourite hobbies.

Though I had written the government of British Columbia, where free schools were flourishing, asking for advice, and had received most encouraging replies, we still managed to make many mistakes. The two worst, I think, were our policy of admitting all-comers and our almost total lack of structure. There were too many things going on at once. The noise level was always very high.

For me, at least, the emotional strain, the worry, the responsibility with which I was most reluctantly saddled, was far worse than any financial drain. Selling all your goods and giving to the poor is easy enough. It's a different matter when you have to give yourself as well, become a full-time worker, trying on the one side to keep the institution from self-destruction, and on the other side from being trampled by the forces of law and order.

Some of our students had emotional problems. Some had severe social hangups. Many were embittered by the hostility of parents and teachers and the adult world in general. A few had drug problems. By then there were students with drug problems in every high-school in Newfoundland, but only in our case was the blame placed on the school—I suppose because we tried to help them with their problems instead of merely turfing them out on the street because of the barest suspicion that they might be smoking grass, as was the universal practice elsewhere. The idea that students, as well as adults, might have the right to due process had not yet penetrated the minds of the so-called educators in the vast majority of high-schools of that time.

In spite of the lack of professional counselling (or, perhaps because of it) we managed to help straighten out some problems, and even to reunite students with families from which they had become estranged. In some cases those most deeply embittered began to lose their bitterness. Those who had always been taught to believe they were worthless gained one of the greatest of all personal assets—self-confidence.

If I were doing it again I'd try to make admissions less easy. No school, no matter how free, can really afford to take all-comers. We were also too permissive about casual visitors, those who came to satisfy their curiosity and had no intention of staying. We were too permissive about noisy social activities in a space too small and in rooms that lacked any kind of soundproofing. We failed, except intermittently, to control the "crasher" problem. We simply lacked the physical means to keep people out of the building after it was supposed to be closed for the night. And we were, unfortunately, almost next door to a public barroom. Things were littered, of course, but relatively clean. Students swept and even scrubbed. Neither people nor dogs relieved themselves on the floor, as happened at Rochdale in Toronto.

Perhaps because our students came to the idea of free education at too advanced an age we spent more time than we should have plodding through the curriculum established by the government and patterned on ideas out of the nineteenth century. We spent too little time exploring the real riches of human culture. Ideally, a free school should have its own resources, as widely based as possible, from which its students could choose what they wished, certainly not "social studies" texts written by teachers who might or might not be able to teach, but who emphatically do not know how to write.

In spite of it all, Animal Farm was a great success. No one who attended failed to be enriched by the experience. Teachers from the regular school system came visiting, talked, perhaps for the first time, with friendly, happy, relaxed students, and went away lamenting that the spirit of Animal Farm could not be introduced into their own schools. Even from the narrowest point of view, we helped twenty students pass public examinations that otherwise they might not even have attempted. But our greatest success was with the one hundred others who had their high-school work behind them, or who had no interest in completing it. People from widely different backgrounds learned something about one another. Students from some of the more "privileged" homes in the city mixed successfully with street kids and learned how to share their experiences. We had some success in teaching caution with drugs and encouraging people to seek medical help if they really needed it. No other school in St. John's had any success at all in this respect, because no other school was based on trust and mutual helpfulness. Such ideas might be put forward in other schools by teachers who wished it might be so, but when you came down to it the schools were based on force, compulsion, and, all else failing, an appeal to the police.*

I learned something from the experience myself—something I already knew in theory, because it was older than Christianity. It is this: if you set out to befriend the underdog, to help those in need, to work for the good of others, you do so at your peril, and must accept the danger that you will be sent to prison or assassinated. There were, in fact, several attempts by the police between 1968 and 1971 to find the means of putting

---

* One Roman Catholic school warned its students against trusting the police, and brought upon itself a deluge of public condemnation.

me in jail, but I wasn't shocked by this, because Joe Smallwood had tried it earlier. Like my predecessors the ancient prophets I was stubborn about serving god in my own way, but the one thing nominal Christians will never forgive is the actual practice of those principles to which they give lip service.

Among the Animal Farmers extremes of dress were *de rigueur*, perhaps as a means of identifying themselves to other members of the New Culture, as it was called. Long hair and bare feet were very much in style, all the more so because both were absolutely banned by the "straight" schools. Those who couldn't hack going barefoot went to the other extreme, and affected work boots. For a while, bellbottoms were almost universal, but soon gave way to blue jeans. Maxi-skirts had only a brief vogue, because in fact they tend to be a great nuisance, but many young women adopted fancy garb that might have come from the property boxes of touring theatre companies. Love beads flourished only briefly. You'd see students with such bizarre ornaments as necklaces made from the pull tabs of pop cans, or fancy hash pipes hanging from leather thongs. Beaded rings and bracelets were popular. All of this was symbolic of the fact that students weren't soldiers or prisoners, to have their personal lives ordered by The Man. One professor at Memorial actually tried to make male students wear neckties. They reacted by going to her lectures in bare feet; one even wore a piece of rope instead of a belt.

The revolt over dress was more than just a fad. Dress codes were symbolic of the students' status as serfs. Many public schools demanded uniforms, often including coat and school tie. If the school uniform was not enforced, then girls were allowed only the plainest colours such as navy blue with white tops. All this was the very sign and symbol of the social constipation of the sixties, a social constipation that the dropouts were sworn to relieve. So bare feet *were* important, despite my failure to explain this to some of my friends. In one panel discussion at Memorial University I was asked why long hair seemed to matter, and was struck by an inspiration: "It's the outward and visible sign of an inward and spiritual grace," I replied, to the great delight of several nuns who were present, and who recognized this quotation from the prayer book.

Perhaps the intelligence level at Animal Farm was very high—I don't know, but I do know that we proved brainy students don't need to be spoon-fed in schools. Robert's average score was 82% in the public exams, but that was by no means the highest in the school. One young woman would have won a government scholarship with the highest marks in the region, except that students at private schools were excluded by regulation (otherwise they would have walked away with all the scholarships, year after year). Another, who refused on principle to write the public exams, was admitted to Memorial University on her general record. A third, who did the last two years of high-school in a single year at Animal Farm, was admitted despite missing the prescribed mark in math by a point or two. (I met this young woman again, some twelve years later, doing post-graduate work at the University of Waterloo.) One boy who couldn't write essay-type papers made a near-perfect score in math. He later owned his own computer company, and wrote programs that netted him a small fortune.

The drug scene was, of course, heavy—not nearly so much at the school as in the community at large. By 1970 the "hard" drugs, the narcotics, were still uncommon, and cocaine was not yet the expensive fad that it became once the yuppies arrived. But cannabis, LSD, mescaline, DMT, STP, psilocybin, among other "soft" drugs, were circulating in St. John's. At least, mixtures were circulating under those *names*. The mixtures were often so impure that dealers began selling a special product called "clinical acid"—real LSD, not a mixture of methadrine and various other mind-benders as so much "speedy acid" turned out to be when analysed.

Out of a hundred or so regular users of soft drugs (mostly grass and hash) whom I knew personally, there were four who might be described as compulsive or habitual users. One was a married university graduate who used LSD or other pills every week, and often more than once a week. He said himself that his ability to concentrate and do demanding intellectual work had suffered, but he had never had a bad trip, and had never made any effort to stop using drugs. He seemed not to be physically affected except for being more or less permanently stoned.

A younger man who dropped out of college through lack of interest though he had abundant ability told me himself that he thought his IQ might have dropped from around 140 to around 100. (Such a drop is not irreversibile; the sharpness of the mind gradually recovers if drugs are discontinued.) This man had tried speed and so on, but used acid as a regular thing, often in "runs" several days consecutively. He didn't believe he had a problem, and invented various reasons why he should continue using LSD. He'd "swear off for a month to get back into shape" only to go out and get stoned again the next night. His behaviour was exactly like that of an alcoholic, in fact.

The third, also with high IQ, smoked grass the way others smoke tobacco—first thing in the morning, then several times a day for years at a stretch. Whether the drug had anything to do with it or not, he had several psychotic interludes, some of them very severe, spread over twenty years or so, but also went for long periods completely normal.

Most bad trips ended only in mild depression. I saw little else that could be described as serious damage. Even three of the heaviest users I knew later had children who seemed to be normal in every respect. The flap about "broken chromosomes" that the anti-drug campaigners tried to use in the early 1970s was just a scare campaign, with no basis in human experience or clinical history. My own complaint about the drug generation is that so many of them turned out to be even more rigid conservatives than their parents, and sometimes were every bit as destructive in their relationships with their children as their own parents had been. This, however, was by no means a general rule. Many of those who renounced the ways of their parents in favour of a broader humanity have remained all their lives committed to peace, non-violence and human values.

Before leaving the subject, I should state that the police behaved very badly indeed—not the members of the RCMP who raided my house at Beachy Cove on two occasions, and tried to make out a case that I was contributing to delinquency; they may have behaved stupidly, but they were at least professional—it was the members of the Newfoundland Constabulary, the downtown police in St. John's, who acted like the hooligans that they actually were, under their neat uniforms.

They came bursting into the school on various occasions, usually at night, and usually without any excuse whatever. Once they came searching for a runaway girl that they had no reason whatever to suspect we were hiding. They came searching for drugs which they had no more reason to suspect on our premises than on any other school premises in the city. They never found anything. They smashed the door into our study room rather than opening it in the ordinary way—it was never locked— whether for psychological effect or from mere vandalism I was never sure. They tried to browbeat the students, but not when I was present. They did all their dirty work behind my back because, like many others, they were afraid of my influence with the press and the media, and the connections I had with powerful people in St. John's and Ottawa. John Turner, who later became prime minister, was one of those who wrote and offered help. Geoff Stirling, the media millionaire, contributed money. The head of the RCMP drug squad had been called on the carpet in Ottawa after raiding my house. But when my back was turned they might do almost anything.

Their worst action was to sieze an epileptic who was having an attack on Water Street near our front door and to throw him in the lockup. When one of our students went to the head of the detachment and explained that the guy might die in his cell, they got frightened and took him off to hospital. There they waited until he regained consciousness, and tried to badger him with questions about drugs until they were stopped by a doctor.

I suppose such things were no more than normal for the times. It was a period when harassment of visible minorities was widely approved and regarded as one of the normal duties of the police in the service of the middle-aged WASP establishment.

How much has changed in the past thirty years? I'm not sure. Students have won the right to due process, even to being represented by lawyers, if necessary. Dress codes are more lax than they were; young people are even allowed to look a bit outrageous, if they wish. Soft drugs are socially acceptable, even if they are still technically illegal. Hardly more than cosmetic changes, these. The fundamental struggle for human liberation has not progressed very far. Overt racism is no longer popular, but First Nations people in Canada still have trouble gaining even their legal rights under treaties, much less acceptance as first-class citizens. Is there such a thing as social progress? Yes. But the movement is glacially slow.

Chapter 7

I knew none of the literary lions during their cubhood. Before I ever met them they had all achieved some notable success. Alice Munro had already won the Governor General's Award. Margaret Laurence had published *The Stone Angel*. Margaret Atwood had won the Award for poetry and had published *The Edible Woman*. Though she already had a number of poetry collections behind her, it was the novel that was the true harbinger of her extraordinary success.

By 1970 the great Canadian literary renaissance was under way, though we didn't realize it at the time. The inauguration of The Writers' Union in 1973 was right on time to catch this great flowering and to become a major part of the nation's cultural awakening. It was the coming together of writers prior to organizing the union that led to my meeting with such people as Robertson Davies and Pierre Berton, then at the height of his fame with the series of railway books. Indeed, if the union had done no more than bring writers together at the annual conventions, that would have been justification enough for its existence, but of course it has done far more: it has made writing a high-profile profession, improving both the morale and the bank balances of its members. It also raises and discusses issues that otherwise would never be addressed.

The first time I remember Atwood, except for seeing her at a meeting, we were sitting somewhere outdoors on the grass in Toronto, and we talked, among other things, about *The Edible*

Margaret Atwood

Woman, which had become something of a cult book among the feminists, but had languished in Jack McClelland's stacks for a year at least, until Margaret got the Governor General's for poetry, and Jack realized that he might possibly have an unpublished best seller sitting on his shelf. She had to remind him, by phone, that it was there. Things like that happen with unpublished books. My own first attempt at a non-fiction book, written at the request of an American publisher, was simply lost by the publisher, and never recovered. A Doubleday editor once told me that they had a registered package of manuscript disappear in the mail between New York and Toronto.

The Edible Woman turned out to be an excellent opening for Atwood's career as a prose writer, attractive to some women, threatening to some men—but male reviewers and critics who were dismayed by the emergence of women writers, front and centre in our literature, already felt threatened by *The Circle Game* and her other poetry collections, though *Power Politics,* the one where the battle lines were really drawn, would not be published for another two years.

She told me that when she wrote the novel she had never heard of anorexia, and thought she had invented the idea of a young woman who was unable to eat for psychological reasons. Fiction is sometimes prophetic, or at least oracular. It was the first of her novels that was "right on" when it came to a public issue. The timeliness of Atwood's fiction cannot be mere coincidence, but I have the impression that it is an unconscious conjunction with a public issue that is just waiting to be born.

A few years later I was closely associated with Atwood in a professional way when we were both officers of the Writers' Union and participants in the cultural politics of the 1980s at a time when we began making the government at Ottawa pay some attention to the writing community. I was never a close personal friend of hers, but I liked her enormously from the moment that we met, as I did most of the other writers I encountered for the first time in the 1970s. There are just a few exceptions, but by and large Canadian writers are pleasant, generous people, with none of the back-stabbing, none of the cattiness that seems to be widespread south of the border. I think it was Brian Moore who remarked that Canadian authors didn't feel the need to be heavyweight champ. Instead, we share a feeling that we are journeying together to the City of God.

Margaret Atwood, in the days when her reputation rested mainly on her poetry, was often compared to Sylvia Plath. If you actually talked with the reviewers and academics and readers who made this comparison, they'd be forced to admit that Atwood had none of the self-pity that was Plath's principal stance—that in most important ways they were poles apart. And in my opinion (I'm in the minority, as usual) Atwood is as far beyond Plath as Shakespeare is beyond Marlowe.

I thought, if you had to compare her with some other poet, she was much closer to Emily Dickinson than to Sylvia Plath—indeed, that she was Dickinson's close successor, though fortunately better armoured to survive in the world. She was not born with the armour; she created it out of necessity. But she was not tough, cruel, or "going for the jugular" as some critics liked to say. Underneath the necessary armour she was more human than most of us, and always willing to expend herself for those needing her help. She was deeply touched by the world's wrongs, and tried to do something about them. As I write this, she's still trying.

In fact, like many other famous Canadians, including Margaret Laurence and Alice Munro, Atwood is a kind, generous, outgoing person, much more equipped to make friends than enemies, and better able to deal with them. In the end, the enemies could be ignored; the friends never were. The people who talked about going for the jugular and all that crap were usually men, and some men, for personal reasons I could never understand, found her threatening. Good Lord! *Atwood threatening*! What kind of men were those?

I think I first met her at one of the preliminary meetings of writers a year or two before the Writers' Union was organized. I remember one such meeting hosted by the Ontario Arts Council and attended by perhaps twenty or thirty writers. There may have been two or three such gatherings altogether. She was already separated from her first husband and was living with Graeme Gibson, one of the young Turks of the *avant garde*. Her marriage had lasted five years, better than the standard three-year marriage among the smart set of those times. She remained friendly with her former husband, an academic named Jim Polk. Gibson's first book, *Five Legs*, was cast in traditional form, but was something of a sensation nonetheless, and was a forecast of his lifelong concern for the environment and the world of nature.

Atwood and Gibson have not only had a long personal partnership, including parenthood, but have made common cause in numerous other ways as well: natural and environmental concerns, sponsorship of social reform, left-wing politics, cultural politics, and such international causes as PEN and Amnesty International.

Graeme's second novel, *Communion*, was so far from traditional fiction that it failed to attract any but the fringes of

Canadian readers. It was rescued from oblivion in the 1980s when McClelland and Stewart republished it as a sort of annex to a new edition of *Five Legs*. Graeme had meanwhile published *Perpetual Motion*, a big historical novel set in rural Ontario, dealing with the extermination of the passenger pigeons, among other themes. I'd hoped this novel would set him firmly on his feet (as *The Wars* did with Timothy Findley) but critics and juries failed to agree with me. Though he later published another big novel, *Gentleman Death*, he remains one of the most neglected of major Canadian writers.

Graeme Gibson

Graeme has been very effective in cultural activities. He was the driving force in organizing The Book and Periodical Development Council and The Writers' Development Trust, as well as the union. In all these activities, Atwood backed him up. She was also very effective as a cultural lobbyist, expert at taking the right minister out to lunch in Ottawa whenever we needed support inside government for some policy vital to the welfare of the writing community.

At about this time Margaret had also published her first novel, *The Edible Woman*, and had been adopted by the feminists, who have continued to do their best to hold on to her, though she often gives them a hard time. The truth is that Atwood has little patience with bullshit, whether it comes from men or women, and not much sympathy for people who blame the failure of their careers on the prejudices of editors and reviewers. If you want success, you have to go for it the way she has, not just sit back and wait for it to come to you, but in her case the success overlies a serious, committed artist, who well deserves every honour that she has collected.

I liked the way Margaret was female, rather than feminine: she never painted her face, never wore "sexy" clothes, never gave the impression of a sex object. I always thought of her as a colleague, a partner in the great game of creating Canada, and I rejoiced in her success as I'd rejoice in that of any member of my own family.

I appreciated the way she always picked me out, the few times we met at public readings, and made it clear that we belonged to the same club. On one occasion at St. John's this doubtless added to the resentment that the academics and literati already felt towards me, because she simply disappeared with me, instead of drinking cocktails with those gathered to lionize her. She doesn't drink in any case, so skipping cocktails was no great sacrifice. Instead, we visited the few things in St. John's that are worth visiting, including a retailer selling handicrafts. She was delighted with Newfoundland double-knit wool mitts, something you can't get anywhere else, and bought pairs for friends as well as for herself. Twice she did readings at arts festivals in Annapolis Royal, and on one of those occasions I had the pleasure of taking her to visit relatives in the Annapolis Valley—because, of course, she is a Nova Scotian by descent, with a line of overachievers in her family.

There have been many different views of what the artist is or ought to be, the view that she should be serving the social good, the view that any "messages" should be sent by Western Union, the view that the artist is a seer pointing humanity toward divine truth, the view that the artist should serve the currents of his time (as, for better or worse, he usually does) and the view that art deals with realities far beyond the purview of mere science or philosophy. This last is a favourite of the artists themselves; they love to imagine that they have a divine mission to explain humanity to itself. But in the end most such seers keep repeating Carl Jung and Jesus and Plato and, if they are on a high level, the Prophet Isaiah. "This above all, to thine own self be true," as Shakespeare said, speaking through the mouth of Polonius. A good motto for any artist, but Herman Melville may have put it even better: "Keep true to the dreams of thy youth." Difficult enough for any artist to do, given the pressures of editors and publishers.

Poets and other artists are regularly canonized and then ignored. Especially, perhaps, in the United States, where artists have been very few, and very far from the policies of the state. But in Canada too. It was typical of Can-lit in the 1970s that the media picked out a few artists to be idolized, and then totally ignored what they had to say. So with Margaret Laurence; so with Margaret Atwood. A phrase here and there, out of context, is used for propaganda, but the artist as a seer, as a prophet, as a potential saviour, is neither heard nor heeded. Most of all, this process is promoted by television, which is never interested in what an artist has to say, but only in how she looks, what kind of "image" she projects, whether she can be treated as a sibyl or some other magical object. Insofar as any attention at all is paid to what she says, it is made to fit into the current categories of the journalists. She is either a "feminist" or she isn't. After that, everything must fall into place. She may be, like Thoreau, a sworn enemy of the state, but that's neither here nor there. Her views on all major issues can be ignored, so long as we can focus on one small aspect of her work that's "newsworthy," relatable immediately to some popular category with which the public is assumed to be familiar.

An example of instant false popularity occurred when Constance Beresford-Howe, a master of satire and an established novelist of great skill, published *The Book of Eve* in 1973. She was immediately hailed as a leader among feminists, but these same people dropped her like a hot potato when she published *The Marriage Bed* in which feminists were shown with wry satire acting and talking the way the more extreme feminists so often do.

Of course, Margaret Atwood is a feminist, as Laurence was, and as Munro is. But if any of them were asked about this outright, they would hesitate before answering, not wishing to be confused with the characters in *The Marriage Bed*. Atwood would have nothing to do with the crazies on the fringe who were always trying to co-opt the movement as their own. Munro puts it this way: "I'm a feminist about certain measures that I would support. But if it's defined more broadly as an attitude to life which is imposed on me by someone else, then I don't accept that."

I asked her if she felt that she had suffered discrimination by editors and critics because she is a woman, and she answered bluntly, "No. I don't."

All this would be equally true of Atwood. Anyone trying to define her life as a feminist struggle is going badly astray. The kind of discrimination her work sometimes suffers is that encountered by anyone, man or woman, who is simply too successful. She has often had a mixed reaction from her peers. She was passed over, time and again, when she published novels that might well have won Governor General's Awards before finally receiving the award for *The Handmaid's Tale* in 1985. Bill Percy, who was on the jury that year, told me that they were unanimous about it—no other book was really in the running. It is not unusual for major writers to be passed over for such awards. Mowat—unchallengeably the major non-fiction writer in Canada, has received the Award only for a children's book.

Many of her colleagues were silent when Atwood was signally honoured. When I met her and congratulated her about a week after she received the Molson Award she said, "Harold, you're the *first person* who has offered me a word of congratulation."

Why? There may be a feeling that anyone so successful as Atwood must, on the face of it, have sold out to commercialism. It's not rational, but you hear it expressed sometimes. Also, I suspect, there is a false feeling that she is unapproachable.

Few of her literary fans are aware that Atwood is a political writer, as well as a poet and novelist. She once collaborated with the anarchist George Woodcock on a biography of Prince Peter Kropotkin, one of the anarchist "saints." She has published studies of the communist parties of Yugoslavia and Canada, and a book on the CCF-NDP in federal and provincial politics. She is a frequent contributor to the slightly-left-of-centre and slightly-feminist-leaning journal *This Magazine*, a journal that deplores the drift toward the right by the New Democrats.

Other women writers that I admire include Gwen MacEwen and Alice Munro, but I never had a close enough association with either of them to have a lot to say about them personally. I did manage to spend some time with each of them while I was writer-in-residence at the universities of Waterloo and Western Ontario (I was also influential in getting Atwood and Marian Engel to Waterloo for lectures, readings, and seminars).

Gwen MacEwen

Gwendolyn MacEwen was a poet of rare depth and sensibility, widely admired among writers who were not poets themselves, but who knew excellence when they saw it. She was also a talented fiction writer who has never received due praise either for her early fantasies, such as *Julian the Magician* and *Noman*, or for her great historical novel, *King of Egypt, King of Dreams*. If MacEwen had chosen to celebrate women characters in her fiction and poetry she might have made a hit with the feminists and sold a lot of books, but she chose to celebrate men. Her principal male characters ranged from Julian in 1963, through Pharaoh Akenaton in 1971, to T.E. Lawrence in 1982.

She was an expert historical researcher, and also a linguist who made herself familiar with modern Greek, and with such abstruse subjects as Hebrew and Egyptian hieroglyphics. She probably knew more about the religion of the Canaanite Hebrews than many a Biblical scholar. I once asked her if she had ever made up her mind about the relationship between Akenaton and his successor, Tut-ank-Amon. Instead of answering at once, she laughed, and said, "You're the only person in Canada who would ask me that." Then she relented, and added, "They were certainly related in some way. Tut could have been a younger brother or a nephew. We'll likely never be sure."

Munro, like Atwood, is a stable, self-directed person. Gwen was not. She was unstable, dependent, alcoholic, but a genius. She was the sort of neurotic who would walk up six flights of stairs because she didn't trust elevators; the sort who would find herself unable to work, frequently attached to the wrong kind of man, often losing her way, appealing to colleagues for moral support, frequently desperate for money. None of us would have been surprised had Gwen committed suicide, and in the end her self-destructive use of alcohol came close to it.

I did Gwen MacEwen one small service which seemed quite important to her at the time. Late in her career when she was broke and didn't know where to turn, I alerted a friend of mine to her plight, and that friend (who admired her work but didn't know her personally) made her a substantial gift of cash, which was about the only useful thing you could do for her at that time.

She had a very unhappy life, and it ended in darkness, but she left behind a legacy of great writing.

Everyone I know admired Alice Munro's writing from the time she published her first collection of short stories in 1968, but my own admiration stems in part from having watched her develop in technique and in depth as she matured. I always enjoyed her fiction, but there was a stage in her career when it seemed rather repetitious. That ceased with a great advance in her middle years. It is both uncommon and gratifying to see a fiction writer improving as she grows older.

Alice Munro

I had rather limited contact with her because, unlike Atwood, she was never active in public affairs or cultural lobbying. I sometimes joined her and the fiction writer Larry Garber for lunch at the University of Western Ontario while I was writer-in-residence there and Larry was in the English Department. Alice usually came to town from her remote abode in the back country once a week. I can't remember, though, that we talked much about writing. It was later, at the University of Waterloo, that Alice and I got to talk about our craft, the origins, the times and places, the reasons for it. I had never done this with either Laurence or Atwood, and I regret, now, that I didn't.

Alice was born in the kind of place to which she eventually retreated when she was already established as a fiction writer. Wingham, Ontario, her home town, was neither a quaint little hamlet nor a place of any importance. It was one of those drab, featureless, crossroads towns with a population of two or three thousand in the middle of the featureless farm country of southwestern Ontario, some twenty miles east of Lake Huron. She began writing at the age of eleven (as I did) and, like me, she thought at first that she was a poet. This may be so with quite a few prose writers, and it may be a very good thing indeed: poetry is an excellent entrance into the difficult world of style, and all too few Canadian writers have anything to recommend them as stylists. Perhaps they missed the enriching experience of reading and writing poetry when they were teenagers. Prose tends to come later in life, just as it came later in human history.

With Alice, the prose began about three years after the poetry. She had been making up stories in her head since she was a child. Then, in her mid-teens, she began writing them down because she thought they'd be easy to write and she could sell them to *Chatelaine* for lots of money.

"But the money wasn't all that important, really, because I was a girl, and girls weren't really expected to earn their own living outside the home. The real reason for the stories was to create some part of the wonderful world I had found in books. At first I was content to live in other people's stories. Then I wanted to create a piece of this imaginary world for myself."

She published her first story while still a student at the University of Western Ontario. Robert Weaver took two of her early pieces for his CBC literary program, and later published some others in *Tamarack Review* (the sheet anchor of many a Canadian fiction writer in the 1960s and 1970s.) The first time she saw one of her stories in print was in *Mayfair* in 1953. She also published in *Canadian Forum*, where you got to see yourself in a literary environment but weren't paid anything. Trying to be a fiction writer in Canada in the 1950s was not much better than trying to be a poet. The short story was badly out of fashion, and Canadian writers still weren't supposed to exist. When, as a student, Alice encountered her first adult Canadian writers, she was astonished that there really were such people. She had thought all serious writers in the English language lived in the United States, Great Britain, or Ireland.

She was strongly influenced by L.M. Montgomery, but then, Montgomery wasn't a mainline Canadian writer; she was a writer of juveniles with a thoroughly international reputation. Alice related instantly to Montgomery's Emily books, *Emily of New Moon* being a girl who is determined from childhood to be a writer and nothing else. Alice was surprised to learn that Emily had been such an influence on me, as well.

"Weren't you bothered that she was a girl?"

The question had never crossed my mind. To me, Emily wasn't a girl. She was a writer, trying, in a rural part of Canada, to create herself out of nothing. And the picture of her struggles in *Emily Climbs* was just what we all believed we had to encounter between the time we sent out our first manuscripts to *The Saturday Evening Post* or the *Ladies' Home Journal*, and the magic time when we held a first book in our hands.

But perhaps *Wuthering Heights* was an even greater influence than Emily. Alice was enthralled by the descriptive parts, and actually memorized some of the speeches in that wildly romantic novel, like an actor with Shakespeare. But though Emily Brontë was a romantic to the core, this didn't seem to affect Munro's thoroughly contemporary realism. She may have written some flighty romantic stuff in her youth, but she was thirty-seven by the time she saw her first book in print, and by then a fully developed writer. Indeed, the book appeared at the invitation of an editor at Ryerson Press, who had seen her stories in *Tamarack Review* and *The Canadian Forum*. There may be some early romantic stuff in her archives at the University of Alberta, where there are rumoured to be "failed" Munro stories, but if so she hasn't authorized publication.

To Alice's utter amazement, *Dance of the Happy Shades* won the 1968 Governor General's Award for fiction. It was almost unheard of for this to happen with a first book, much less a book of short stories.

"But the books didn't sell," she told me. "Even after the award they didn't sell." Ryerson was a reliable publisher for serious Canadian writers, but was not known for selling a lot of books. Then Ryerson was bought by the American publisher McGraw-Hill, and there was a howl from Canadian nationalists that here was another wicked American corporation gobbling up a small Canadian publisher. But the wicked Americans did a bit better than the Canadians. Munro's book was republished as an attractive paperback, and things improved.

The attitude of Canadian reporters toward women writers in the 1960s is illustrated by the headline in the Victoria paper, where Alice was then living with her husband: "Mother of Three Wins Award," it announced. She was also amused by the *Globe and Mail's* description of her as "a shy housewife."

With her fourth book, *Who Do You Think You Are?* published in 1978, Alice moved to Macmillan because she wanted Doug Gibson for her editor. She says Doug is not only a good editor, but is also concerned about a book's appearance: he is careful and meticulous, interested in such things as the cover and the blurbs. When Doug moved, seven or eight years later, to McClelland and Stewart, Alice moved with him. It's the only instance I know of an author following an editor from publisher to publisher.

Munro was never one of those writers who believed you needed an income and a "room of one's own" before you could write. She was always doing the housework, getting the kids off to school, then grabbing a few hours to spend at her writing on the kitchen table or any other place where there was room to park a typewriter. She wrote *Lives of Girls and Women* in the laundry room because the laundry machines kept it warm, and if she got "blocked," as most writers do from time to time, she could always tell herself that in reality she was doing the laundry. Later, she worked in her bedroom.

She wrote most of her first drafts, and seconds, and thirds, on a typewriter, but in the early years she did a lot of travelling by train, and always wrote in longhand between cities. She even did such writing in a roomette on transcontinental trains, between Ontario and British Columbia. I, too, wrote extensively on trains, both local and transcontinental. Such unlikely people to have such parallels!

After moving west with her first husband, she spent twenty years in Vancouver and Victoria, and that was where her children grew up. But she was never really at home there, was always planning to return to rural Ontario, the place of her roots and the background of her fiction. She not only returned to Ontario in the 1970s, but to the rural southwest, to Clinton in the middle of the snow belt, about ten miles east of Lake Huron, and equidistant from the cities of London and Waterloo, practically a twin to the town where she lived as a child.

"I love the land," she told me, "though *love* isn't the word. It's like this place is part of me, like my own flesh, or something," adding ruefully, "unpopular as I am here."

Her unpopularity, if it still exists, must stem from her refusal to be just another small-town housewife, and especially, perhaps, her refusal to write like a shrinking violet. Alice's writing is not exactly robust, certainly not in the least bawdy, but she lives in a part of the country which never got out of the 1950s, a place about ten times more puritanical than Halifax, and twenty times more conservative than St. John's. In Clinton, as in Wingham, women's work consists of baking, quilting, tatting and embroidery. Alice is regarded in rural Ontario as a sort of middle-aged Tomboy, not quite a Real Woman, a disgrace to her sex. Bad enough if those stories had been written by a man—but what can you expect of men? Because a woman wrote them, they were condemned twice over. Her books were removed from school reading lists in her part of the country, just as was done with Margaret Laurence's books in Peterborough. Unlike Laurence, who was devastated by the reception of *The Diviners* in her home town, Alice remained quite unaffected—what could you expect of school boards, after all? Nevertheless. That such major fiction, so innocently expressed, should be treated like this in Canada is, of course, a national disgrace, like our treatment of the people of the First Nations. My own novel *White Eskimo* was at first ordered by the thousand for use in Newfoundland schools; then the order was cancelled because the Roman Catholic school board objected to it.

We have much to be proud of in this country, and much to make us squirm.

Chapter 8

While I was writing my second and third novels, organizing Animal Farm and defending it from the police and the lynch mob, I was also working part-time for *The Evening Telegram*. For a period of between two and three years at the end of the sixties, convinced that I was now past the danger of being destroyed by journalism, I went back to feature writing, working at it two and a half days a week. The experiment was not very successful. I have always needed direction from an editor before I decided to work on a major piece of journalism. Perhaps *The Telegram* thought I was now too high-profile for this, and tended to use me as a kind of captive VIP. In any case, I found myself all too often with nothing to do. Before the end of 1969 1 had decided to cut myself from newspapers once and for all. At the same time *The Telegram*, following its purchase by the Thomson chain, had decided that I was a disposable luxury. So at the end of that year we parted on friendly terms. Steve Herder and I remained friends for the rest of his life, and he gave me every possible assistance when I needed material from his files for a book I was writing. I was planning to move to Ontario in the spring or early summer of 1970, and had no specific plans to return to Newfoundland.

That winter, to work on the first draft of *White Eskimo*, I left my house at Beachy Cove to the flower children and the rock band that was then calling itself Land of Mordor—the same, more or less, that later evolved into Lukey's Boat. I took my typewriter, lots of warm clothes, and a few books to a summer cabin on the shore of Healey's Pond, about four miles away, renting it from its owner in St. John's.

The cabin was a delightful place in summer, with a stretch of lakefront, a wharf for a boat or canoe, lots of mixed hardwoods and evergreens, and a long array of windows facing south across the water. Unfortunately, since the builder had not expected it to be used in winter, it had no insulation, no storm windows and no adequate heating. To be comfortable at night I had to curl up in my eiderdown sleeping bag, a five-star Arctic from the Woods corporation, and by day I had to work at a card table within a few feet of the little oil stove, the only source of heat in the big living room. To keep it going I had to carry oil in small drums from the road. But despite such handicaps—or because of them—I worked extremely well, and was quite happy, as I always was, when a major piece of writing was going as it should. In two weeks I completed first drafts of eight or ten chapters. There were no distractions to interrupt the work—no radios, TV, record player, newspapers or telephone. For entertainment I'd knock off work on the novel to write a short story, or walk through the snow to the wharf to sit on bare boards warmed by the midwinter sun.

To make it tolerably cheerful indoors I set out a dozen pots of hyacinth bulbs along the southern window sills, these being a sort of plant that would not be damaged by the cold. They burst into bloom, and filled the place with perfume that competed, more or less successfully, with the fumes from the oil stove. Nobody except Robert was supposed to know where I was. Once or twice a week he'd arrive late in the afternoon, and we'd cook a chicken on the little two-burner stove, and celebrate with a bottle of wine. But in spite of the fact that I was in hiding, two of the local kids at Portugal Cove located my retreat, and walked all the way for a visit. Gordon Harvey and Terry Picco, eleven or twelve years old at the time, shared my supper and made thorough nuisances of themselves for two or three hours, then, in the darkness of night and the dead of winter, departed on the four-mile walk back to their homes. Aside from Robert, they were my only visitors, but CBC did find out from him where I was, and sent a crew with TV cameras for an interview. By then, fortunately, the hyacinths were in bloom, and made a great background for the film.

Now and then I'd go to Beachy Cove for a look around, and by midwinter I had decided that I had to move back there to save the house from being wrecked or burned to the ground. The flower children had put a fist through an antique stained glass window which I was never able to replace, had broken the quarter-ton hearth stone by cleaving firewood on it, and had smashed the cast iron brackets of my two antique wall lamps in the sitting room. I threw them out (both hippies and lamps) and went back to working for a few weeks in my own house. But at the beginning of summer I let the house out for rent, and moved into Farley Mowat's cabin a few miles east of Brighton on the shore of Lake Ontario, where I wrote the second draft of *White Eskimo* in temperatures that often reached 100°F. Writing about sled journeys in the Labrador winter seemed to make the heat more tolerable. I swam in the lake every day and worked outdoors whenever the mosquitoes allowed it. Midday sun drove them into the shadows; mornings and evenings they were intolerable. Never in Newfoundland or Labrador had I encountered mosquitoes worse than in southeastern Ontario, both on the lakeshore, and along the Rideau waterway.

Indian Summer, as Farley called his cabin, was a sprawling bungalow on an acre of lawn and marsh and scrub surrounded by trees. It had a well that produced brown water from a nineteenth century hand pump worked by rods and levers. A note pinned to the wall assured guests that this water was quite drinkable when mixed with rum. The pump broke down, and I had to use a system of pulleys rigged to the trees in order to get the massive contraption out of the well for repairs. There was electric power in the cabin, with a refrigerator and stove, an oil heater (another antique, which I also had to repair) two small bedrooms, an enormous living room with double bed, a small kitchen and a "working cabin" that I did not use at all.

I spent many hours weeding out and restoring perennial flower borders that had not been touched since Farley's mother had lived there about ten years earlier. I dug the thistles out of the lawn, and planted trees in all the gaps along the fence lines to make the grounds invisible to neighbours in case Farley still wanted to run around *au naturel*. There was excellent swimming a few yards away at the lakeshore, with limestone ledges from which you could dive into water that looked quite clean.

A mile or two inland, on the bank of the canal that connected the lake to the Bay of Quinte, lived a family with whom Farley had been friendly—the Van der Toorns, part of the very small Dutch community in eastern Ontario. Ari and his wife Elizabeth became good friends of mine. Their eleven-year-old son Johnnie came weekly to trim the half acre of lawn at Indian Summer, and went swimming with me in the lake, or accompanying me on long bicycle rides. Tom and Helda Buck occasionally came from Toronto for a visit. Margaret Laurence's cottage on the Otonobee was an hour or so away by car.

She and I would spend weekends together at the one place or the other. She was then working on revisions to *The Diviners*, and, like me, suffering from loneliness because she felt she must spend at least four days a week in uninterrupted labour if she was to get her monstrous manuscript into publishable shape.

I sometimes took Johnnie Van der Toorn and his younger brother Gary to The Lake on the Mountain overlooking the Bay of Quinte, or to some other swimming beach, and once or twice to Toronto to visit the islands, the exhibition grounds and Ontario Place. Occasionally I had visitors from St. John's. Leslie McGrath came to spend a week. Robert came for a few days. But such visits, spread over three summers and autumns, still left me alone for long stretches. At Beachy Cove and Animal Farm I had grown so used to mobs of people that five or six days without visitors made me feel neglected.

During my first summer there I bought a bicycle, the first I had owned in twenty-five years. It had a Straumey-Archer three-speed rear axle, adequate for the hills of southeastern Ontario, and I did a lot of cycling between bouts at the typewriter. I'd cycle from the cabin to the provincial park at Presque-Isle, for example, tour around the park, perhaps swim in the lake, then cycle home—twenty miles or more all told. I often cycled five miles to a supermarket in Brighton, and brought home my bag of groceries in the luggage carrier. From Brighton I would take the detour along the Great Pine Ridge, which involved a couple of miles riding uphill, and the same coasting down. I sometimes rode to Trenton and back as well. Once I was really in shape I must have averaged thirty miles a day. The bike had rubber pedals so I rode it barefoot, and often with my shirt tucked into the luggage carrier. I grew lean and brown and healthy that summer, getting lots of exercise, skipping lunch and eating only two modest meals a day. The Van der Toorn boys would ride with me to Carrying Place or Brighton. Few adults, as yet, rode bikes, but almost every boy in Ontario owned one. Some kid swimming at the canal one day remarked to me, "Bicycles are anti-pollution machines." I don't know where he picked up the slogan; it would be another fifteen years before the Canadian public began to take any real interest in saving the environment.

I continued to ride my three-speed for eighteen years. Then, in the autumn of 1987 my son Andrew bought a European mountain bike, and it proved to be such a wonderful machine, so superior to all previous kinds of bicycles, that I bought one too (a cheaper model than Andrew's), and have used it a great deal, riding on the hills and valleys and dykes of Nova Scotia.

From the cabin at Brighton the manuscript of *White Eskimo* went off to my editor, Doug Gibson, at Doubleday, and I was able to turn my attention to yet another book that Doug had put into my hands. This was the manuscript by Cassie Brown of St. John's with the title *Death on the Ice*. Not to mince words, this manuscript was so badly structured when I received it as to be unpublishable. Cassie had done a great job of research on the *Newfoundland* sealing disaster of 1914; in my opinion, the research couldn't  have been better, but she had no idea of how to go about writing a book. She had submitted it first to McClelland and Stewart, who had rejected it out of hand. Then, at my suggestion, she had sent it to Gibson at Doubleday. Doug at once realized that he had a potential winner on his desk, provided the book was completely rewritten by a professional. He said he'd accept it and sign a contract if Cassie would get me to help rewrite it. I agreed, and since Cassie owned a motel at Donovans near St. John's, she offered me a cabin in which to work on the manuscript.

Cassie Brown

ROYAL PHOTO SERVICE

At that time I had no place of my own in Newfoundland. I had rented my house at Beachy Cove to Mary Jane Payne, the young woman who had organized and was then running the first alternative food store in St. John's—a small business that was soon to develop into the largest alternative food store in Canada. She was a good friend of mine, and of Robert's (who by now was old enough to have girlfriends) and I had helped her a little with the organizing and financing of the store. I saw her occasionally in Ontario when she drove to Toronto to load her van with cheese direct from the factory, whole grains from grain processors and Chinese goods from the wholesalers.

So while I had lots of places to visit—Mary Jane at Beachy Cove, Leslie McGrath in her house at Horse Cove, my nephew John and his girlfriend in their cabin at Beachy Cove, there was no place where I could settle and work. I therefore accepted Cassie's offer to work at Donovans in a fully serviced cabin with shower, refrigerator and electric range. With such services at hand, I had absolutely nothing to do but work on the book and cook the occasional meal. Once again, except for Cassie and her staff, Robert was the only person who knew where I was staying, and he came to visit two or three times a week. I sometimes had dinner with Cassie and her sisters in the big dining room of the motel. On average, I could work at *Death on the Ice* fourteen or fifteen hours daily.

From what I knew of Captain Abram Kean and his associates, and with the help of a book of his that I owned, I was able to add a little to the information in Cassie's manuscript, and especially to round out the picture of Captain Kean's character, which was central to the story. A great uncle of mine had been one of Kean's subordinates on the critical voyage described in the book, and my father knew something about their relationship. Kean, it turned out, was a fascinating character, a ruthless man with strong puritan morality, always willing to risk men's lives to make a profit for himself and his employers. He would have been at home among the whaling masters of New England. Basically, the information was all at hand. What I had to do was rewrite the book as a rapidly unfolding drama, to pull the reader into the story and to get the sealers to the ice pans as quickly as possible. To do this I had to scrap the long introductory chapters that Cassie had written, and start the story on the deck of the ship as she steamed northward into the ice.

It was not at all difficult. By the time I had rewritten the first half of the book I found that the story was moving along well. Apart from tightening the style a bit, there was little work needed on the second half. I retyped the whole thing, added a short forward, a prologue like a trailer to a movie, and had it in shape and retyped in a mere two weeks.

Because the work had taken so little time, I told the publishers that I wanted only ten percent of the royalties (I could have had fifty percent, which would have netted me, eventually, about fifty thousand dollars) but even at that the book was such a success that I have been well paid for my two weeks of intense work. I was convinced it would be a best seller, and told Doug Gibson so. He and Doubleday were over-cautious. They ordered 5,000 copies, and had to order a reprint less than a week after publication. Sales in hard cover and paperback ran quickly into the hundreds of thousands and continued for many years. Thirty years after publication it was still selling 3,500 copies a year.

Unfortunately, Cassie Brown did not realize how utterly rare it was for a Canadian book to sell like that. Consequently, she was much disappointed by the modest success she achieved with her two subsequent books, both of them well-researched, well-written, and well-reviewed, with sales that most Canadian authors would envy.

Not content with publishing two best sellers in 1972, 1 also brought out, that year, a volume of poetry by four young Newfoundlanders with introductions that I had written for each—*Voices Underground*. I put this book together because I wanted to introduce the young poets to the public, especially

140

Drew McGillivray and Des Walsh, both of whom had begun writing poetry while full-time students at Animal Farm.

Some of Drew's poetry I had literally salvaged from the floor or out of waste paper baskets where someone had tossed it while cleaning up. Des was more careful with what he wrote, but required much more encouragement, more assurance that it really had merit, because he had received no encouragement either at home or at his former school. Des later became a well-established poet and literary man, a central figure in Newfoundland's cultural renaissance.

The poetry in *Voices Underground* is quite exceptional. I took it to my friend Jim Bacque, who was then editor and publisher at New Press. I went to another friend, the artist David Blackwood, for a cover picture. He loaned one of his beautiful bleak engravings, and also produced an original colour engraving for the dust jacket of *Death on the Ice*. Unfortunately, New Press chose a colour combination for the cover of *Voices Underground* that tended to spoil the effect of Blackwood's picture, but by the standards of new poetry the book sold, anyway. I think New Press ordered a thousand copies. By the following spring the printing sold out, and they reordered, but the additional copies arrived so late that the demand had dried up. New Press was itself in trouble, and General Publishers eventually took it over. Nevertheless, *Voices Underground* showed up in six out of ten libraries surveyed for public lending right in the late 1980s.

I found a small press to publish Des Walsh's first poetry collection, and to save expense designed it myself, with cover and illustrations by the talented young artist Ellie Cohen (my wife's eldest daughter, who won two first prizes in two categories of the Newfoundland Arts and Letters competition that year). I also helped Des to get his first Canada Council grant, with such outstanding referees as Andreas Schroeder and Margaret Laurence, both of whom admired his writing, and from there he went on his own. His poetry production has never been large, but is of the highest quality. He has published four collections to date, has written plays, edited a magazine, collected folk songs, and scored an enormous success as senior writer of the TV drama *The Boys of St. Vincent's*, which collected more international honours than anything previously produced by CBC-TV. He also wrote the stage adaptation of *Tomorrow Will Be Sunday*, which was successfully produced at St. John's twenty-five years after the novel was first published, and later a film script for *Random Passage*.*

Drew, much to my disappointment, gradually stopped writing—indeed, seemed to have lost the gift for phraseology and imagery that he so clearly had at the age of fourteen. This, I'm told, is often the way with poets who blossom very young. Leslie McGrath told me the same thing had happened to her: she could never again write so well as she could while still in high school.

After the great success of *White Eskimo* I decided to turn away from traditional fiction, from novels that looked like some minor effort by Conrad or Lawrence or Laurence. Whatever the publishers might wish, there was going to be no *Son of White Eskimo* or *White Eskimo Returns*. Instead, I took up once again the book that eventually became *Remembering Summer*. It was then going through draft after draft under such names as *To Toslow We'll Go*, *The Toslow Fire Sutra*, and *Visits to a Magic Parlour*. (What titles! Wish I'd had a use for them all!)

I worked at it in the winter of 1972 and through much of 1973 with unsatisfactory results. I showed it to several editors, but none was able to make a constructive suggestion, with the

---

* First novel by a former student of mine, Bernice Morgan, who scored a great success with it, and published an equally good sequel, *Waiting for Time*.

exception of Jim Bacque, who pointed out that Eli was the most interesting character in the book, and ought to be given much more play. Consequently, on my next rewrite Eli came straight into the foreground and stayed there.

It would have been no trouble to find a publisher for a "drug book" or a "hippie book" in 1969. Indeed, several such books appeared from Anansi and other small publishers, and must now be something an embarrassment to authors who have graduated from that kind of thing to Can-lit's centre stage and numerous awards. What I was doing was something quite different, but at the same time it suffered from the total rejection of the sixties that took place in the seventies.

After Doubleday had accepted the book, I had second thoughts myself. I went back to Doug Gibson and said, "Look, this book isn't ready for publication. I want to take it back for one more rewrite, and when I'm ready to publish I'll go to a small literary press. That's where it belongs. Instead of doing the third novel that I've promised you, I'll write a biography of Captain Bob Bartlett, the great ice captain who took Peary to within spitting distance of the North Pole." He agreed, and I began work on *Bartlett*.

I also sent *Remembering Summer* to McClelland and Stewart with one of the strangest letters ever sent by an author to a publisher. "It would not be right," I said, "to deprive you of the opportunity of reading this unpublishable book." They, too, failed to give me any useful advice, or, if I remember correctly, any advice at all. You'd think I was an aspiring "hopeful" with his first novel, instead of a solidly established writer who had just published two of the most successful books of the decade, and was here attempting a landmark novel unlike anything that had been published in Canada before.

My first venture into biography wasn't easy, either. Fortunately, the Newfoundland archives had obtained from Bowdoin

College in Maine photocopies of Bob Bartlett's papers, which included his logs, his notebooks, many of his letters, and numerous pages of typescript for books and articles that he had worked on but never published. This saved me a trip to Maine, and the expense of staying there while I sifted through all this material, deciding what needed to be copied. Some of the photocopies at St. John's were so bad as to be difficult to read. Bartlett's handwriting slowed me down to a crawl, and the handwriting of his brother Will, his first mate, I found to be virtually illegible.

The secondary sources were of little help. Most of what had been written and published about Bob Bartlett was drivel. I had to work directly from Bartlett's manuscripts and books. Fortunately, he wrote voluminously. Even his original manuscripts—those from which his ghost writer had worked—were available in fragments, and proved to be far better written than the published versions. The "ghost" who had worked both for Peary and Bartlett tended to reduce everything to respectable dullness. Bartlett had also started to write the story of his childhood and youth, but had abandoned the job, leaving a pile of typescript that had never been published. It brilliantly illuminated his early years in Brigus, helped to explain his relations with his difficult family, and supplemented my interviews with his nephews and his brother Will, all of whom had sailed with him on his later voyages.

There were serious contradictions in some of the various versions of stories that Bartlett had told over and over again, in lectures and in print. I concluded that he had built up the anecdotes from one lecture to the next, and that the version to be trusted was most likely the first one. Worse than this was a collection of ships' logs in Bartlett's handwriting, leaving the impression that he had been present on voyages that he had nothing to do with, as I was later able to confirm from the dates. After much puzzlement, I discovered that the logs were those of ships commanded by other members of his family, and that he had probably been planning to work on a family history.

Fortunately, I was able to rent a large loft-like apartment within an easy walk of the Newfoundland archives and the downtown public library. Then, whenever I came up against problems that puzzled me, I could drop the typing and resume my research. I had the good fortune not only to be able to interview Will Bartlett at length while his memory was still strong, but even (amazingly) one of Bob Bartlett's teachers, a nun who had taught at Brigus in the nineteenth century, and was then living in a convent at St. John's, nearing the age of 100, her mind and memory still perfectly clear.

I required documentary research in archives other than those at St. John's, but here, again, fate conspired to make the job as easy as possible: the university of Western Ontario, straight out of the blue with no lobbying on my part, asked me to spend a year there as writer-in-residence. It so happened that one of the documents I needed to consult was a doctoral thesis that existed only in manuscript at that very university. What's more, they gave me an office right next door to the library, and the library was able to obtain for me, free of charge, printouts of everything I needed from the national archives at Ottawa.

My luck with *Bartlett* continued. Ernest Chafe, the last survivor in Canada of the *Karluk* expedition, gave me a manuscript that he had written a few years earlier. Chafe was bedridden and near death at the time. Another year, and I would have been too late. When I had finished with Chafe's manuscript I lodged it, as he had asked, in the Newfoundland archives. Then—my luck continuing—while I was revising my next-to-last draft the very last survivor from the *Karluk*, a retired scientist from Scotland whom I'd assumed to be dead, since he was now in his nineties, published his own account of the expedition. William Laird McKinlay's views were at variance with Chafe's, though they both regarded Bartlett with veneration. McKinlay turned out to be a rather cranky correspondent, and he was clearly wrong on some of his historical points, but his account added colour and anecdotes that I could not have collected from any other source.

Lastly, I learned that a member of the Soviet Academy of Sciences had published an analysis of the final polar expeditions by Peary and by Dr. Cook in the light of scientific evidence that had accumulated since the Second World War. By good fortune I was able to obtain an English translation of this most important paper.

All those elements coming together just at that moment enabled me to do a thorough, in-depth study of Bartlett's character and career. It was the last possible moment, so to speak, when the book could be written from various living as well as documentary sources. If it had not been for the problems with *Remembering Summer* I might have postponed Bartlett for another five years, and consequently the book would have been much poorer. As St. Paul is reputed to have said, "All things work together for good to those that love God."

I was disappointed by the sale of *Bartlett*, which appeared in 1977. The original press run of 5,000 took more than a year to sell out. Much to my surprise, I discovered that this great man would continue to be ignored in mainland Canada. The book went into paperback for another modest sale. Doubleday did not reprint it until 1989, but it has been in print ever since. When they reissued it in a revised edition it had a new and more attractive cover, and has been selling in recent years at the rate of about 500 copies a year.

Compared with *White Eskimo* and *Death on the Ice* it was not especially successful, but Doubleday assured me that they were happy with the results. Between the publication of *White Eskimo* and *Bartlett* the Canadian hardcover market had collapsed. Trade books had become too expensive for most private buyers, and there was (still is) an annual spate of trash from subsidized publishing houses, making it all the more difficult for real writers to reach readers, or for real books to gain proper attention.

Bartlett had been more than four years in the making, leading me to resolve not to tackle another biography. Meanwhile, there were a couple of easy books that required almost no effort.

Only the Gods Speak, my short story collection, consisted of pieces that I had written purely for my own entertainment, with no specific plans to publish. I had placed one or two of the stories in *Queen's Quarterly*, and in the annual anthologies published by Oberon. One had been commissioned by Rudy Wiebe for his collection, *Stories from Pacific and Arctic Canada*. Some critics called it the best piece in the collection. It was republished in Denmark, and later in the People's Republic of China, but Canadian anthologists refused to touch it because it showed Inuit boys using "cuss words" and smoking grass. When one anthologist wrote me asking me to bowdlerize it for school use I didn't even bother to reply.

I was not ambitious to be a short story writer, and certainly had no wish to bombard the literary journals with short fiction. The book was published simply as a place to preserve a few extraordinary short pieces, each of which was intended to be judged solely on its own merits, and all of which clearly belonged in some time and place other than the dreary literary scene of Canada in the late seventies, where fiction had become little more than the dismal account of the day-to-day lives of dull and boring middle-class people.

I had begun writing fiction in the first place as a revolt against the cult of the anti-hero. I wanted a novel that I could enjoy reading, not one that bored me, and since almost no one seemed to be writing such novels, I decided to write them myself.

Hence Eli and Christopher and Virginia and Joshua Markady in *Tomorrow Will Be Sunday*, and Gillingham in *White Eskimo*. My short stories, too, were written in rebellion against the stuff then being published. Though there were exceptions to the lusterless norm of Canadian short fiction—the Cape Breton stories of Alistair MacLeod, for example—such exceptions were few. My short stories not only had exotic backgrounds—the Arctic, the Caribbean, landscapes of vision and dream—but also aimed for colour, character and mythological qualities—stories filled with caviar rather than gruel. Because I was writing for fun I could indulge myself; I used a little of everything: magic realism, surrealism, fable, parable, allegory. One or two reviewers complained that the book was a mere collection, that it lacked a "theme." Indeed, that's exactly what it was—a collection, and why should any story collection have a "theme?" I enjoyed doing my own thing in a period when almost everyone else was imitating Margaret Laurence and Alice Munro with precious little success. Theme indeed! I wasn't writing for reviewers or the Can-lit establishment or Governor General's juries. Though I wouldn't have said so in public at the time, I felt such trendy writing, such a pitch to second-rate readers, to be beneath my notice. ("I strove with none, for none was worth my strife" as Walter Savage Landor said.) In fact, I have always written against the trend, convinced that I knew exactly what I was doing, and that the rabble was doing what the rabble has always done, peddling imitations and secondhand ideas.

Another easy book was *Beyond the Road*, a short essay with interviews, illustrated by a wonderful portrait photographer, a young American named Stephen Taylor, and published by Van Nostrand Reinhold in a beautiful edition. Taylor made the work easy for me by doing taped interviews with many of the people he photographed on Newfoundland's Great Northern Peninsula, and securing transcripts of the tapes. I supplemented some of his interviews with my own, for I knew the Northwest Coast very well indeed, added a running commentary, and pasted the book together. The portraits—in which you look straight into the eyes of the subjects—are enduringly beautiful, and by themselves are a splendid analysis of the character of those outport Newfoundlanders. The text is a further analysis of the nature of sudden change in a primitive society. I reread it several years after it was published (the first time I had ever reread one of my books) and was delighted. It is one of the few things I've written in which I wouldn't change a single word.

At about the same time Harry Cuff—an old friend of mine, and a small St. John's publisher—asked for permission to collect and publish a group of Labrador Indian tales that I had originally published in *The Newfoundland Quarterly*. The tales were collected and translated into English by Innu high-school students at the native school in Northwest River. I had added a commentary. The little book cost me no effort whatever. All I had to do was write a letter saying, "Go right ahead." Once a year, for perhaps ten years, a small royalty cheque arrived, and I used it to buy a bottle of rum.

Starting in the seventies, I wrote or co-authored a number of potboilers that I do not propose to discuss here, except to record the fact that I wrote them to keep meat and potatoes on the table while I did far more important things like building a new house, adding two greenhouses, and creating a piece of parkland where nothing but a hayfield had existed before.

Those books included a volume in Jack McClelland's history series with the title *The Colonial Dream*, dealing with Canada from the Cabot voyages to the fall of New France; a complete short history of Canada from the voyages of discovery to the patriation of the constitution, written for an American package firm named Bison Books, and two volumes dealing with pirates, outlaws, bandits and privateers, co-authored with a former student of mine, Ed Butts of Mississauga. Those books fall into the same category of writing as my magazine articles. They are hardcover journalism for popular consumption, professionally done, but in no sense "creative non-fiction," rather, writing that neither required nor deserved the meticulous care and effort that went into *Remembering Summer*, or *Bartlett*, or my later non-fiction essays *Dancing on the Shore* and *The Magic Ground*. They served a purpose, nonetheless. Some reviewers pointed out that this was the first time anyone had specialized in the violent, colourful side of Canadian history. It hadn't been just Louis Riel and the RCMP after all—we, too, had had our wild west (and wilder east). A few parents and teachers wrote to thank me for history books of a kind that kids could read without being bored to death. The second volume went into two mass-market editions by separate publishers, and is still in bookstores twelve years after first publication.

But after all that "hard cover journalism" as I called it, some of my most ambitious writing still lay ahead.

Chapter 9

In 1970 the government of Ontario appointed a Royal Commission on Book Publishing. At that time Ontario was the only province with a significant book publishing industry, and it seemed to be threatened by American takeovers. Gage Publishing, mainly concerned with textbooks, and perhaps for that reason of special interest to Canadian nationalists, had been bought by an American firm. Ryerson Press, of special interest to creative writers, was also taken over by McGraw Hill. McClelland and Stewart, the largest Canadian-owned publisher, was in financial trouble, but had resisted the temptation to become an American branch plant.

Publishers and booksellers were invited to the commission's hearings, but the only writer consulted was the commission's chairman, Richard Rohmer, a lawyer and a writer of thrillers. Rohmer was a distinguished man, Queen's Council, Distinguished Flying Cross, Brigadier-General commanding the Air Reserve of the Canadian Armed Forces, but he did not have a high profile among the writing community, and was not considered by other writers to represent their views.

Farley Mowat, at this point, suggested to a group of other writers that they should attend the hearings of the commission uninvited. His friend Max Braithwaite, novelist and essayist, put together a brief, and it was supported in person by a representative group of writers: Ian Adams, Margaret Atwood, Fred Bodsworth, Harry Bruce, June Callwood, Hugh Garner, Gwen

MacEwen, Graeme Gibson, David Godfrey, David Helwig and, of course, Farley Mowat.

When they presented their brief, Rohmer said to them, "What you need is a union." A sound suggestion; the only national writers' organization at that time was the Canadian Authors Association, which had an open membership consisting mainly of amateurs, and was not very effective as spokesperson for the professional writing community. Mowat and his friends adjourned to a nearby tavern, and began to discuss means of putting an organization together.

They continued to meet from time to time, and to invite others to join them. Out of those meetings the Writers' Union of Canada came to birth following a gestation period of three years. By 1972 they had asked the Ontario Arts Council to set up a formal meeting of Canadian book writers. It was held in December of that year at the Ryerson Polytechnical Institute in Toronto. I was one of the twenty writers there, the only one from Atlantic Canada.

That meeting was really the foundation of the union, though we still had no formal structure. It began to emerge, however, the following year at a meeting in Neill-Wycik College, Toronto, financed jointly by the Canada Council and the Ontario Arts Council. Some eighty writers attended, this time from across the country. Margaret Laurence, meanwhile, had returned from England, and was asked to become "interim chair." She was actually quite unsuited to the formal duties of a chairperson, but was held in such high esteem among the writing community that her nominal position would be bound to attract both members and government support. As it turned out, she never had to chair a meeting.

F.R. Scott, lawyer, poet and constitutional writer from Montreal, chaired the meeting at Neill-Wycik, and a subsequent one in Ottawa, at the National Arts Centre, where the union was formally launched. Scott provided a skeleton constitution, which was debated, amended, and adopted clause by clause. Together with the by-laws, which I drew up and presented a few weeks later, this became the union's formal structure, and has remained basically the same ever since.

A quarter of a century earlier I had been a successful union organizer, chairman of the largest local of the Newfoundland Federation of Labour, and also of the powerful Building Crafts Council. In later years I had been an officer of the Newfoundland Confederate Association, had been elected to the Newfoundland legislature, and had been a member of both the Newfoundland press gallery and the national press gallery at Ottawa. I had also framed the constitution for the Newfoundland Federation of Fishermen. All this experience in union practice and parliamentary procedure was of use to the union when I came to the job of helping to organize it. By a stroke of good luck I was also one of the "high-profile" writers of the time, with three recent bestsellers and two major awards. It gave me the leverage to influence the founding convention, and the union's first critical years.

I may also have contributed to its eventual welfare by fighting to establish the annual dues at the comparatively high rate of $100 a year, instead of the $10 that many members at first preferred. I believed that higher dues would give us a funding base, and help to establish us as a professional organization, not a mere assembly of amateurs. My motion passed. The Canada Council was impressed, and from that time forward we received generous subsidies.

At the founding convention Marian Engel was elected to the chair. Rudy Wiebe and I were joint vice-chairs. This provided a good geographical spread among the officers—Rudy from the prairies, I from Newfoundland, Marian from Toronto. The other members of the first national council were also widely representative of the country at large: Graeme Gibson, Toronto; Terrence Heath, Regina; Robert Harlow, Vancouver; John Metcalf, Montreal; George Payerle, Vancouver; Heather Robertson, Winnipeg; Andreas Schroeder, Mission B.C.; Ray Smith, Montreal and Cape Breton; Kent Thompson, Fredericton. We had so framed the constitution that at least three members of the national council would always be from "the regions." As it turned out, the union always had an excellent distribution of both officers and national council from all parts of Canada. This was important because there was a good deal of regional jealousy,

Marian Engel

Rudy Weibe

Harold Horwood

especially in the west, and a feeling that Toronto tended to dominate national and cultural life unfairly.

Throughout this whole period Graeme Gibson was the most active organizer, and did a great deal to get the union on its feet, though he didn't become one of the officers until 1974, when he was elected to the chair. During that first critical year Marian Engel, Rudy Wiebe and I were the troika that ran the union's affairs. We held regular weekly meetings by conference telephone. Marian did more than anyone to put the union on its feet, and to accomplish its greatest single work, persuading teachers, librarians, and the Canada Council all to back the drive for public lending right, a program that pays writers for the public use of their books in libraries, puts millions of dollars into their pockets annually, and helps to keep some of them from penury. It was a slow process. We won support bit by bit. But by the time I became chairman in 1980 I was able to assure the membership that PLR was on the way. I knew this because the Canada Council was now fully committed to the cause, and it was just a matter of getting the government to vote the money. There was, however, much detailed work to do on the structure—the collection of data and the distribution of the funds. After PLR was already accepted in principle, this detailed work, which took years to accomplish, was undertaken by Andreas Schroeder, and he eventually got much of the credit which by rights should have gone to Marian Engel.

I was elected vice-chair for the second time in 1974, and for the third time in 1979, the year when the union experienced its first major crisis, precipitated by a decision of the national convention to revise the dues structure from the flat fee of $100 a year to an income tax, graduated not to earnings from writing alone, but to the total earnings of the individual member.

Margaret Laurence headed the faction that secured this change in the by-laws. She deeply resented the fact that deans of

155

English and academic vice-presidents who had published a book or two, and regularly earned four or five times as much as real writers, could enjoy membership in the union for a fee that in their case amounted to peanuts while full-time writers such as herself had to pay their hundred-dollar fee by installments.

When this proposal was sprung on a national convention, the motion passed, and a few "real writers" such as myself, Margaret Atwood, Farley Mowat and Pierre Berton (to mention only four) were suddenly faced with paying dues at the highest level along with the deans and the vice-presidents. Most of us stuck with the union anyway, but other "real writers" who didn't sell a lot bore only a small fraction of the financial burden. A whole raft of high-income people, including not only academics, but also historians and other non-fiction writers whose books were selling immediately resigned.

RANDY HAUNFELDER

June Callwood

June Callwood as chair, and I as vice-chair, worked like dogs, writing letters and making phone calls, trying to keep the union from falling apart completely. But the principal stroke of policy was a notice of motion that, at the next annual meeting, I would move to restore the dues structure to a flat fee. We made sure our supporters were there to vote for it, and the motion passed. I became chair, with Atwood as vice-chair and designated successor.

Margaret Laurence, her friend Adele Wiseman, and two or three others then resigned, but the union was more than restored to its former health. Membership increased, and has continued to increase ever since. As I write this, income from membership dues is close to a third of a million dollars a year.

That was the end of Margaret's influence with the union, but she and I remained friends until the end of her life. She was, however, more isolated then formerly, more involved with academic and social issues than with writing, and treading a darkening path. During my year as chair I had the able and enthusiastic assistance of Margaret Atwood as vice-chair, and an able office staff of four people, including a retained solicitor, Marian Hebb, who became the only lawyer in Canada specializing in the problems of the writing trade.

By this time we had organized the Writers' Development Trust and the 1812 Committee, a powerful lobby group that succeeded in reversing the government policy of cuts to the arts, in establishing the image of Canadian culture as a labour-intensive industry (coining the phrase "cultural industry" which had not been used previously) and were conducting throughout the country reading tours that added substantially to writers' incomes, especially those young in the profession. A volunteer committee was doing the preliminary work that led to the establishment of a reprography collective to license the reproduction of copyright material.

At the end of my year in office union membership had passed 500, and we were firmly established as perhaps the most powerful organization in Canada's cultural life, exceeded in this respect only by the Canada Council.

Though the union started as an organization of prose writers only, poets who had not published a book of prose were admitted in 1983.

One other service I rendered the union during its early years was the production of a book of rules for conducting meetings. This little volume, based on parliamentary procedure, was adopted by both the Writers' Union of Canada and the Periodical Writers Association of Canada as a means of bringing some kind of order to annual meetings that had previously tended to be chaotic. It is not specific to writers' organizations, but is a guide that could be used equally well by any small or medium-sized body for procedure at conventions and general meetings.

Apart from services to the union, I also tried to be of assistance to members of "the tribe" who were down on their luck and seemed to be in danger of quitting. I wouldn't have done this for just anybody, but I did it for talented writers who seemed to be in danger of quitting. Out of the blue, I'd write a letter of encouragement. One of them told me she was in hospital seriously ill when my letter arrived. Another said to me, "You, too, must know what it's like to be down on the floor." In fact, I never had been. I'd been successful from the day I started. But I knew that writing, anywhere, is a difficult enough career to tackle; in Canada, with its small population, its crazy geography, and a mob of Americans next door regarding us as their captive market, it is especially daunting.

Two writers that I tried to help in this way later won Governor General's Awards for fiction, and a third was short-listed. I had less luck with poets, though I did get one or two to resume writing after they'd quit. I was especially pleased with Rienzi Crusz of Waterloo, who told me that he'd quit writing, and only took it up again because I urged him to do so. Rienzi has still not achieved the kind of fame he deserves, but his writing is above and beyond the general run of what passes for poetry in Canada, and often wins awards. Published by such small presses as The Porcupine's Quill and Tsar (Toronto) his books are a unique and beautiful contribution to the literature of our country.

I think it is important that people who can enrich the national culture should be encouraged to do it. Real writers should continue to write, even if they seem to themselves to be talking into the wind. Among real writers writing is not a game of sales and prizes and publicity, however hard the media may strive to make it so. Most real writers would rather write their "ten true words" than ten successful volumes of Harlequin romances. And should there be a Henry David Thoreau in our midst (unrecognized, of course) I think the few of us who even suspect his presence should do what we can to see that he doesn't turn into a mere jotter of nature notes. He may not be a "great writer" like Louisa May Alcott, but he shouldn't simply fall silent. Sooner or later, what he says may change the course of human history for the better.

I have had a few such words of encouragement myself. David Lewis Stein, for instance, was going to bat for *The Foxes of Beachy Cove* long before it had graduated into mass market paperback. Thirty years later, when I published *The Magic Ground* and it sank like a stone, I had an enthusiastic letter quoting some of its best passages, and a phone call from another writer telling me that it was her top favourite of all books ever published in Canada. Even if you only sell 289 copies of your beautiful first edition, that kind of thing is enough to keep you going.

The union's activities since the early 1980s have often been in directions that did not interest me greatly. I had deep sympathy with the effort to get an even-handed deal for women writers (and academics) but the uproar from "writers of colour" about "appropriation of voice" and the demand for special treatment (because of some degree of non-European ancestry) left me completely unmoved. I searched through the membership lists of the Writers' Union of Canada looking for "writers of colour." By including Métis, people who claimed one Creole grandmother, and so forth, I managed to stretch the number to twenty, in a membership of more than nine hundred. If you wanted to get beyond that you would have to include Latin Americans.

And yet, the union organized an expensive conference to deal with the problems of "writers of colour." If those people had problems it was not because of their "colour" but because they had never learned their trade as writers, and expected special treatment as members of an oppressed minority. This nonsense tended to die away, along with the nonsense about "appropriation of voice," but while it lasted it was given far more attention than it deserved. There are still echoes from the furor: claims that no one except a member of the First Nations has any right to collect their folklore, and so on. Carried to its logical conclusion, this would mean that no woman should ever write a story from a man's point of view, and no member of the Six Nations should ever write a story about a Cree.

The union should have kept its nose out of such matters, and confined itself to promoting the welfare of the writing community as a whole, its relations with publishers and with government, and so on—the aims for which the union was organized in the first place. On the whole, this is what has happened. After a quarter of a century, the union is still pursuing, for the most part, the issues that led to its organization, and with which it has dealt so successfully.

Chapter 10

At the end of the 1960s I spent three years in Ontario, the summers mostly at the Mowat cottage near Brighton on the lake, the winters at Schomberg, north of Toronto. The cottage had belonged to Farley's father, Angus, and after his death to Farley's mother, but it had been used very little for about ten years before I began working there. To my surprise, I didn't miss the sea very much. The public beach on Lake Ontario within two minutes' walk of where I lived had limestone ledges with surf; the water there seemed reasonably clean; the shore was so nearly deserted that a few people actually swam in the nude. Close by was a long stretch of sand beach with a camping park. A canal joining the lake to the Bay of Quinte was just a couple of miles away, and was used for fishing and swimming as well as for boat travel. There was even a fishing village a few miles westward along the shore, where people caught and sold fish that I regarded as practically inedible. I soon made friends in the area, with the kids who went swimming at the lake or the canal, and especially with the Van der Toorns who lived beside the canal, kept cattle and did some farming.

It was at this time too that I met Edna Staebler, and formed a life-long friendship with that gifted prose writer. Edna lived at Sunfish Lake, near Waterloo, Ontario, and as a result of her familiarity with the large Mennonite community of Waterloo County, she produced a series of cookbooks, spiced with paragraphs of creative prose, that soon made her financially inde-

Edna Staebler

pendent. But her finest writing went into other books of non-fiction, books such as *Sauerkraut and Enterprise,* and *Cape Breton Harbour.* The latter, describing a visit to the people of Neil's Harbour on the northeast end of Cape Breton Island, published in 1972, republished in 1990, has never had a fraction of its due recognition. It is one of the finest travel books ever written in Canada, a book that captures faithfully the lives of the fishing families, especially the women and children, and that reproduces successfully the delightful dialect of their conversation. It is a true example of creative non-fiction—a genre so rare in this country that most critics and jury members don't even know the meaning of the term.

Edna's reputation among other writers is high. Her friends included Pierre Berton, the Mowats and Margaret Laurence, all of whom admired her skill with prose, but to the public she remained "the cookbook lady." It was not for writing cookbooks (however good they may be, as indeed they are) that she received the Order of Canada in 1996. In her wide-ranging prose works she explored the lives of Nova Scotia blacks, of barge crews carrying newsprint from Quebec to New York, of a Hutterite colony in Alberta, of the Ontario Iroquois, of Italian-Canadians in Toronto, among others—always with sensitivity and insight.

Edna Staebler is not only a fine writer. She is a remarkable person. A middle-aged woman living alone in the country far from the protective society of a city, she welcomed ex-convicts into her house, and endeavoured to help them find their way into society. She also entertained American corporation lawyers fighting a court battle over cookie recipes (*The Great Cookie War*). She was still driving her car back and forth to town and swimming in Sunfish Lake at the age of 94. While I was working at the University of Waterloo and living with vegetarian students, she invited me to her house once a week for such treats as Mennonite bean salad, smoked pork chops, and her own incomparable pina coladas made with creamed coconut and dark Demerara rum. Her cookbook earnings allowed her to be generous: she helped to finance the founding of *The New Quarterly* in 1981, and later provided a trust fund for an annual award to a first book of creative non-fiction.

In the late autumn of 1972, following the success of *White Eskimo* and *Death on the Ice* (but not because of that) I decided to return to Newfoundland, sell my property at Beachy Cove, and move to Ontario permanently. Unlike many who had moved there to find work, I didn't dislike Ontario at all. I found it a comfortable place to live, with many fascinating natural features, especially along the shores of its four great lakes, and with its full share of friendly people.

I was in no hurry. I thought of selling my house in the spring, moving back to Ontario in the summer, meanwhile looking for land on which to build my second house. I preferred the eastern part of the province; I looked at land on the Great Pine Ridge near Brighton, at land on the shore of the Bay of Quinte, with limestone ledges and a small stream, and I looked at the quiet valleys among the rolling hills north of Highway 401. My idea was to buy land, park a trailer on it, and then begin the slow process of building my own house.

Mary Jane Payne (my tenant at Beachy Cove and owner of the big alternative food store in St. John's) offered to load up her van with my books and furnishings, and help with my temporary move back to Newfoundland. By the time she arrived at

Brighton there was already snow on the ground. We loaded the van and the car not only with my possessions, but also with a few hundred pounds of the world's best cheddar cheese from the small cheese factories of eastern Ontario, and with half a ton of Chinese canned food from Toronto wholesalers. Then we started east in a vicious snowstorm of wind and rain. It was bad enough in the car. I still wonder how she managed in the overloaded van. Three days later we arrived at Beachy Cove in late autumn sunshine with flowers in bloom. Mary Jane had already moved her things out of my house, and I immediately moved back in. My long-time friend Cat-Cat was there to greet me.

This animal, the same who had hunted for a living the winter I was in Mexico, and had brought me a vole to welcome me home, deserves something more than a mere mention. He was a big tabby male born in the woods to some unknown mother, and rescued by one of the Reardon men the summer I first moved to Beachy Cove. He grew up in my house, and soon learned to hunt by day, spending his nights with me. He was on speaking terms with foxes, and with the neighbours' dogs, none of whom could intimidate him. One visitor's dog mistakenly thought he could attack or frighten Cat-Cat, and soon had to run for his life, with a chunk torn from his nose.

Cat-Cat quickly learned to distinguish between wild animals and pets. I could trust him with a pet bird, including a neighbour's canary, and even with a pet mouse, Morsel, that used to sleep beside him. He would share his food with a visiting kitten. He was once missing for three days, and was found by one of my neighbours in a fox trap, his leg broken. All the vets in St. John's were too busy to look at him, though I tried, so I bound up the leg myself; he recovered, and grew an exceptionally large paw on the opposite leg to compensate. He walked, ran, and climbed three-legged for the rest of his life.

He also recovered from a bout of rat cancer, a disease that kills many cats. His illness was prolonged; layers of flesh sloughed off one side of his head and face, but in about three months his recovery was complete, and he went on from strength to strength for another four or five years.

Cat-Cat would *talk* to me in cat language—not just the occasional "meow," but a whole range of sounds spread over long passages of "conversation" as we sat together. Visitors were astonished and delighted to discover that "Harold's cat talks to him." When I moved to the second house at Beachy Cove, owned by my wife's family, Cat-Cat moved with me, evicted the resident cat from his role of alpha male, and reigned there until his death at the age of twelve years, when he was "put down" by a vet during one of my periodic absences from the province. Had I been at home, it is possible that I might have nursed him through this painful illness as I had nursed him through the rat cancer several years earlier.

I haven't had the kind of close relationship with any other animal that I had with Cat-Cat. We seemed to understand each other almost like people, and he has never been replaced by the various cats and dogs that have shared my house subsequently.

Bill and Corky Cohen who had built on a rocky hill half a mile from me were then getting a divorce, and Bill had moved to St. John's. Corky (the name is short for Cornelia) Lindesmith owned half the equity in their house. Her equity might have been worth $9,000. There was a mortgage with some sixteen years to run. Bill was paying $500 a month support for their five resident children while they remained in school. Ellie, Rozie, Dennie, Tim and Della ranged in age from nineteen to ten.

The arrangement was later ratified in court, but Bill also offered to pay tuition for any of them who went to college. Rozie later tried to take advantage of this, but found dealing with her father too difficult, and dropped the effort. I then offered her an allowance of $100 a month, and with this she paid all her own expenses except board until she graduated. On $500 a month Corky managed to feed the family, meet the mortgage payments, and put a tiny bit of money in the bank. She picked up a bit of extra cash by working casually at Mary Jane's store. These arrangements continued until I bought Bill's share of the house for $8,000. He said he was "being done" but he agreed anyway. I then took full responsibility for the support of his former family. So in reality, he got out of the marriage "scot free" with $8,000 in his pocket. Every divorced man should be so lucky! He soon married a younger woman, and they remained childless on high-level double incomes until they took early retirement. Bill and his new wife had little contact with his former family. Della, the youngest, always referred to me rather than Bill as her father, and it was I, not Bill, who arranged the financing when she and her husband began building a house in British Columbia—a service I also provided for two of his other daughters.

Mary Jane had meanwhile split with *her* husband without bothering to haggle over terms. As settlement, she got an old jeep, which she traded as down payment for a Volkswagen van. To the surprise of many, her store, which started as a small natural-food store, and then expanded into all sorts of alternatives, was an enormous success. By the time she sold it and moved away from Newfoundland to the USA, then to China, finally to Hawaii, it had become a great and flourishing institution, few of whose customers remembered its starting as a one-woman show in a single room on Duckworth Street. For some years it was the biggest thing of its kind in Canada.

Corky's daughter Dennie was living with my nephew John in a cabin that we had built on a former piece of Reardon land adjoining my place. They lived together for ten years before deciding to start a family. They and their three children are still living at Beachy Cove more than a quarter of a century after they first moved to the cabin, proving that companionate marriages can be as lasting as any others, and that relationships beginning in a girl's mid-teens are not necessarily transitory.

As soon as I was settled, John and Dennie moved from the cabin into my house. Mary Jane had moved to Corky's house as a boarder. I can recall very little from that winter. I did some work on *Remembering Summer*, but not much other writing. I was often at Corky's house, where we drank some wine, smoked some pot, and did a lot of "rapping" with residents and visitors. Sooner or later everybody who was connected with the counterculture showed up there. Some of them were friends of mine, some were friends of Ellie's or John's. Robert and Des came visiting frequently, Leslie McGrath fairly often, sometimes with her two children, Andrew and Diedre, sometimes with the latest travelling freak from abroad—they all seemed to find their way to her when they landed on The Rock. The "boys in the band"—Lukey's Boat—spent a lot of time with us too. As I look back on that period it seems to be one of drift—a period of waiting for something to happen. All the ties with my closest friends (Leslie, Mary Jane, Des, Robert) seemed to be loosening. My house was for sale. I still planned to return to Ontario within a few months.

I changed my plans because Corky intervened. I'd known her in a general sort of way since her arrival in Newfoundland in 1968, but I knew certain members of her family, Ellie and Dennie especially, much better. Now she had become part of my immediate circle, and I began to regard her as the most interesting one of the lot. She was an omnivorous reader, with a surprising store of "useless" information, and opinions on everything. We began to spend more and more time together, often just the two of us with Corky's remarkably human-like dog, Chou-Chou, a cross springer spaniel with a startling gift for imitating human sounds and expressions. Chou-Chou was not only good at driving bears away from campsites, but could be relied upon to carry messages between houses, or even small packages. If Corky ran out of tobacco at my place, she'd send Chou-Chou home with a note, and back would come "the makings."

Both of us enjoyed serious reading, classical music, camping, travel, swimming, boats and flowers. We were both fond of children, cats, and dogs. We were both interested in current scientific theories and discoveries. We both read contemporary fiction. Corky did not share my fondness for mathematics and poetry, but otherwise our tastes were remarkably similar. She was enthusiastic about sex, hated housework, had none of the common feminine fixations on dress or personal adornment. During our long life together she has never owned a dress or worn a piece of jewellery, though she sometimes puts on a fancy jacket.

The summer of '73 was cold and wet. Johnny Van der Toorn and a friend of about the same age (thirteen? fourteen?) came for a visit, and I think it rained every day while the boys were there. We managed to swim across Hughes's Pond once or twice, but did no canoeing or camping until after they'd left, in early July. Then Corky and I and her crowd went camping at Great Chance Harbour—an abandoned settlement in Bonavista Bay that you could reach only by boat or by a difficult tramp through the woods. There were no houses remaining, just clearings, with good beaches and tidal flats, and an exceptional trout pond just over the hill where you could always count on catching a meal of pan fish. We literally lived off the land—trout, shellfish that we gathered almost at the doors of our tents, wild vetch, wild mustard, various species of wild mushrooms that grew plentifully in the woods.

Chou-Chou did her usual good job of driving off bears, but one of them sneaked into camp early one morning while we were still asleep and tore open the back of John's tent right above his head. He and Dennie woke with the bear's muzzle pointing down at them.

"Jesus Christ! A bear!" John yelled, sitting bolt upright. At this the bear hurriedly withdrew. At the same time Chou-Chou awoke and took off after the bear vowing murder in a loud voice. The bear, having barely escaped this encounter, never dared come close to a tent again, but continued to hang about, circling through the woods at a distance of a couple of hundred yards. You could always tell where he was, because Chou-Chou pointed at the spot and barked viciously. It was all great fun, except that one of John's aluminum tent rods was bent out of shape, and there was a two-foot rip in the canvas.

By this time John and Dennie had moved into Corky's house, where Ellie, Rozie, Tim and Della were also living. We did a lot of visiting back and forth, and Chou-Chou continued to shuttle from house to house by way of the Ridge Path, replenishing salt, spices, herbs and tobacco as needed. I had quit smoking tobacco a year before this, but Corky was still rolling her own. Some time after she discovered that she was pregnant, she decided to quit, and went "cold turkey" after twenty-five years of smoking. She had no problem quitting, just the same, and never touched tobacco again. Meanwhile, four friends of mine killed themselves with tobacco.

We were married in St. John's by a retired Presbyterian minister in a truly private ceremony, with just the necessary witnesses.

Everyone arrived for an outdoor party at my place on one of the last sunny days in autumn, and we had a glorious time. It was our last celebration at the old house—on the deck, in the field, in the long, lovely sitting room with its great stone fireplace; we drank a gallon of wine and probably smoked a little pot; Mary

Jane, friend to all of us, showed up with various goodies from her store.

Corky and I were still living in my house at Christmas, and we decorated both houses, mine with a traditional tree, the Cohens' with a tree sprayed all over with black paint. I baked a fifteen-pound dark fruit cake, using a recipe that had come down from my great-grandmother on my father's side.

I was unhappy about moving out of the little house that I had rescued and rebuilt and made habitable, and in which I had written five books to that date—not counting *Death on the Ice*, which I had rewritten at Donovans. But there was no way I could afford to keep two houses going—one or the other had to be sold, and Corky's was far the more suitable for a large family.

My regrets were not all sentiment, by any means. Since the mid-fifties I had been living either in my own house or in my own apartment as sole proprietor, doing my own cooking, cleaning, bed making and so on. Neither Marguerite nor Corky had ever interfered with my housekeeping. Now I was about to move into a house that was already being run co-operatively by a group of young adults. I liked all of Corky's kids, but three of them were grown up, and doing for themselves and for the younger ones all the things that I had been doing for myself and my guests for the past twenty years. For a fifty-year-old "loner" adjustment to this kind of co-operative living wasn't going to be easy. I don't think anyone else realized how onerous it was for me—neither Corky nor John nor her daughters understood what a difficult adjustment I was undertaking. It wouldn't be easy for them, either, of course. Except for his slippers and his glass of Scotch Bill Cohen had never been much of a house person. Having a man in the house full-time, meddling in every domestic chore, would be a new and unwelcome experience for all of them.

Some time after Christmas word got around St. John's that my place might be for sale, though I still hadn't offered it on the market. Lois Saunders (a CBC freelance writer) heard of it and gave me a call. We knew each other, had met frequently, and she had interviewed me for television on location at Beachy Cove, so she was familiar with the house and land.

"I hear you're selling your place," she said.

"Yes."

"How much do you want for it?"

"Twenty thousand dollars if I sold it to a friend. More, if I offer it to the public."

"Do I count as a friend?"

"Of course, Lois!"

"Good. The cheque will be in the mail tomorrow."

"Thanks, Lois. I'll make out a bill of sale."

It must have been the easiest real-estate sale of the decade, all done over the telephone in less than two minutes. And the cheque did, indeed, arrive in the next mail. No agents or lawyers were involved. I delivered the bill of sale personally, and we registered the real-estate transfer at the Division of Deeds in Confederation Building. I agreed to move out in less than a week.

I now had $24,000 in the bank, which made me feel financially secure, at least for the time. I suppose I had spent between $4,000 and $5,000 on renovations to the old house, in addition to the $2,500 purchase price. The trees I'd planted, the root cellar I'd rebuilt, the garden I'd cultivated, the physical work I'd done on the house might add up to another couple of thousand, but about $10,000 was a capital gain, created indirectly by my book *The Foxes of Beachy Cove*, which had made the little place one of the more desirable spots on the outskirts of St. John's.

So in mid-winter I packed my books, took my collapsible book cases, and moved into Corky's house. The transition was even more difficult than I had foreseen, but we survived it, and within six months were adjusted to the new life. Corky never suffered because of a pregnancy, never experienced morning sickness, had no pain—at least no severe pain—during the contractions of labour. Stranger than this, perhaps, her pregnancies didn't show—her hips spread, but her belly remained remarkably flat. Less than a month before she was "due," Bill Cohen visited us to argue about our offer to buy his share of the house. Like everyone else except the immediate family he never suspected that she was pregnant.

That winter Corky went skiing, and slithered up and down over the icefalls that passed for paths between the house and the highway. I almost cracked my skull on one of those icefalls myself, and tried to make her cautious. To mitigate matters as well as I could I installed a thick hand rope from tree to tree so at least there was something to catch hold of so you wouldn't go catapulting over the rocks. If she ever took a fall she didn't admit it, and the baby arrived as he was supposed to, in May.

When it was near time for the confinement I tried to get a doctor to attend the birth at home. No way. They wanted drugs, oxygen, surgical instruments, a monitor for blood pressure, heaven only knows what else, all within reach. They weren't going to be responsible for the unspeakable dangers of a natural birth. Corky wanted to have it at home anyway, and even contemplated sneaking off and having it in the woods, all alone. She'd had too many unpleasant experiences with nurses and doctors insisting on interfering with natural birth in hospitals. Anyway, labour started early in the morning of May 14, before she was fully awake, so much against her will I hauled her off to the Grace Hospital. I wasn't going to be blamed, either, for what might happen.

On arrival, I began to see what she meant about hospitals. She walked from the distant parking lot without help, but once she was inside they put her in a wheelchair. Later, they tried to make her take drugs of various kinds—drugs to assist labour, drugs to deaden non-existent pain, etc. She refused medical intervention of any kind.

"You go on home," she told me. "I'll be perfectly OK. I'm used to dealing with these people."

I went home and waited for a phone call. It seemed a long time in coming. At 4:00 P.M. I finally phoned the nurse on the floor.

"Your wife isn't even in labour, Mr. Horwood," the nurse told me. "We'll call you in plenty of time."

Twenty minutes later, Corky was on the phone.

"It's a boy," she said. "No doctor was present when he was born. The nurse was just fine, though. She stood by and said 'push,' and it was all over in a minute. They've hauled the baby off to a nursery, which I don't like. The baby ought to be with me."

"Hang on," I said. "I'll be there as soon as I can."

Mary Jane had been in touch with me all day, and she now asked me to pick her up before going to the hospital. So we arrived together, and found Corky pacing restlessly about in a dressing gown.

"They can't keep me here, of course," she said. "I've already signed myself out. But they *refuse* to let me take the baby."

"We'll see about that," I said. I got very angry. Mary Jane got very angry. We told them that we were going to take it, whether they wanted us to or not. They pointed out that we couldn't just barge into their nursery—we'd be committing heaven only knows what kind of felony.

"You can take the baby home tomorrow," they said, "if everything turns out right. We have to check the baby's this, that and the other thing; drop silver nitrate into its eyes in case Corky had the clap; feed it on lots of sugar water from a bottle, etc.

"We're taking it tonight," I said. "I'm going to get my lawyer on the phone right away. He'll find a magistrate and get a writ of *habeas corpus*, and we'll have it served on you within an hour."

"And the newspapers will hear all about this, tomorrow," Mary Jane added.

At that point they caved in. I signed papers releasing them from all responsibility for what might happen, and we finally walked away with him three hours after he was born. We took him to Campbell Avenue to visit his grandparents, aunts and uncle, and then headed for Beachy Cove.

He was a delightfully active baby, about eight pounds (much the heaviest Corky had ever had) not only able to "hold up his head" as they sometimes say of newborn infants, but able to take his weight on his feet while you held him under the arms. He was doing just this, standing on my knees on the couch at Beachy Cove four hours after birth when John's dog Eric came bounding into the room barking with excitement and Andrew began to cry for the first time.

Chapter 11

Apart from Ellie, Dennie and John, the person from Animal Farm who became the greatest fixture at Beachy Cove was Katie Parnham. She was a great friend of Corky's kids, interested in all the things that seemed important to the "Aquarians." Eventually she qualified as a specialist in handicraft techniques, and began teaching classes. Not just a constant visitor, Katie was almost a member of the family, and even lived at Beachy Cove for a while when Corky and I were away.

We were doubly connected to the Parnhams. Katie had been one of the young people who helped to hold Animal Farm together; she believed in it and worked hard to make the school succeed. Apart from this, Corky had known the elder Parnhams, Peter and Sheena, almost from the day she arrived in St. John's in 1968. She and Bill had rented a downtown apartment owned by Peter, and later bought a house on Portugal Cove Road from his company. A year or two later they sold it to John O'Dea when they built their place at Beachy Cove.

While Corky and Bill were splitting up, Peter and Sheena were also estranged and living apart. Katie was a sort of surrogate mother to her two younger sisters and her nine-year-old brother, Jonathan, who was at an especially loose end in a family that seemed to be falling to pieces.

In midsummer 1973, after Corky and I began living together, Katie brought Jonathan for his first visit to Beachy Cove, and he promptly decided that this was where he wanted to stay.

An affectionate and demonstrative child, he quickly became attached to me—we seemed to fill a need for each other: our earlier children were now grown up, and the younger ones were not yet born. For about two years, Jonathan divided his time between his mother and me, spending weekends and holidays at Beachy Cove. When his parents finally got back together and went off for winter vacations in the West Indies, they sent him to live with Corky and me.

I took him canoeing, swimming, and fishing. He was instantly successful at trout fishing, and also learned to handle a boat safely. He worked with me on my first building projects at Corky's place. This included putting up walls to enclose the car port and make it into a large workshop where you could build a boat or change the engine in a car, or do any other job that required a large working space. We also added two small bedrooms at one end of the house, building them on a concrete pad. It then became a three-level house with six bedrooms—not one too many considering that ten people lived there much of the time, and there were often overnight guests as well. Everybody knew that Beachy Cove was the centre of The Scene, as it was called in those days.

For his work on the house I paid Jonathan a dollar an hour. He was worth more, but that's what his mother stipulated. Besides driving nails and sawing boards with tireless enthusiasm he also mowed the lawn at my old house (now inhabited by Lois Saunders) and used the money to buy his first good bicycle, a five-speed which he rode up and down the hills between Portugal Cove and St. Phillip's.

Even more than Katie, he became a member of the family, and when the school term ended in June 1974, while I was temporarily working in Ontario, he flew to Toronto to join me. We camped at Pickering, visited Niagara Falls, the Science Centre, Ontario Place, and the museums. Then we drove to the

Maritimes, and went down the Saint John River between Mactaquac and Gagetown by canoe. I was writing a piece on the Saint John for a book, *Scenic Wonders of Canada*, to be published by Reader's Digest, and was covering the river in stages. Everywhere we went we stayed at campgrounds; everywhere Jonathan made friends instantly with other boys, and this usually led to my meeting the boys' parents and sitting around in trailers or tents drinking endless rounds of beer.

Jonathan then flew home, and Corky and Andrew flew to Sydney, where I'd arranged to pick them up by car. About fifteen miles from the airport, and twenty minutes before they were due to arrive, the car broke down, and it was an hour before I could get it going again. Meanwhile Corky paced around the airport terminal with six-week-old Andrew. I tried phoning from a nearby farm house, but the airport people seemed to have no idea of how to get a message to a passenger waiting on their premises.

We drove to the northern border of New Brunswick, where the Saint John River enters Canada from the state of Maine. Then we went camping and canoeing on various parts of the river between the Maine border and the Bay of Fundy. We arranged a small plastic tarpaulin so the baby could lie in the canoe and look up at the sky and the passing clouds without getting sunburned. For safety we had a long nylon cord attached to him, so we could retrieve him if the canoe upset—but of course it didn't upset; I've never upset a canoe. We visited all parts of the river from Glazier Lake to the city of Saint John. The baby loved it. We saw eagles soaring by. We watched ducks. We listened to the lapping of water under the cedar strips and the fiberglass. We were all three very content.

But trouble wasn't far off. I woke up in the tent one night suffering from renal colic. I didn't know what it was. The pain seemed to be in the bladder. It was so bad that I decided I must get to the nearest hospital, which happened to be in Edmundston. There I told the doctor I thought I had a urinary infection. He agreed that I probably did. There was a trace of blood in the urine, but he still didn't diagnose a kidney stone. He prescribed an antibiotic, and warned me that it would turn the urine a very strange colour—a sort of yellowish brown.

We continued our trip until we reached Saint John, and from there drove home to Beachy Cove. I was still having bouts of pain, and I was still taking the antibiotic, though it didn't seem to do any good.

"When these things come on I feel like I'm about to die," I told Corky.

The attacks continued for six weeks. One evening we had a visit from two young hitch-hikers from Toronto, and I cooked a meal including such exotics as marine snails in fried rice. The colic came on while I was standing at the stove, and after I had served the food I went out and lay down between the flower beds to wait it out.

I was still calling it cystitis, and (the antibiotic having done no good) I was back to my grandmother's remedy—sweet spirits of nitre—which, of course, did no good either, except that it may have prevented the stone or stones from being further complicated by an infection.

Leslie McGrath meanwhile had arrived for a visit. Among her other qualifications, she was a trained nurse, and she apparently realized that I had something more serious than a bladder infection.

"I'm taking you to The General," she announced, and we drove to the hospital in the MG sports car that she had inherited from her marriage with Miller Ayre, and which, at that point, still had a few kicks of life remaining in it.

We went through the usual rigmarole at the desk while I sat there in obvious pain, but if you *walk* into a hospital clinic you are supposed to be able to stand the grilling by the staff. They gave me a place to lie down on a cot, and after a while a very young doctor came in and said, "I think you need a sedative." He gave me a tab of Demerol, and then, an hour later, another, and told me I'd see a specialist as soon as possible.

Meanwhile the victims of a multiple crash on the highway had started to arrive, with crushed pelvises, ruptured kidneys, and heaven only knows what else. The specialist glanced at me. I told him I'd been lying there for hours, and the Demerol wasn't working. He gave me a shot of morphine, and went off to attend to the accident victims.

The morphine didn't put me to sleep, or entirely kill the pain, but made it quite tolerable. They moved me into another room, and I lay there all night, my mind drifting. The exhausted specialist came to see me around breakfast time, told me I had a kidney stone, and ordered a set of X-rays.

They took twelve full-trunk X-rays, developed them, found they were out of focus, and then took twelve more. Between the two sets of X-rays I threw up last night's snails and fried rice.

In the afternoon the urologist showed me the pictures, identifying the stone at the juncture between the left kidney and the urinary tract.

"You'll probably pass it," he said. "Urinate through a handkerchief for the next few days, and if you pass the stone you'll see it. Drink lots of liquids. They're useful for flushing. We don't operate unless the kidney is actually threatened. Meanwhile, I'll give you a prescription for Demerol. Take two when the colic starts."

"Any recommendations for the future?" I asked. "Diet for instance?

"Diet is very controversial," he said.

Before I left the hospital I had a talk with the young doctor, who, I suppose, was an intern.

"When you pass the stone, bring it in for analysis," he said. "Likely, it will be mainly calcium."

"Does that mean I should eat less calcium?"

"No. But there's probably something wrong with the way your body handles it. Drink more liquids than you've been drinking—half a gallon a day should be *minimum*. And one other thing. Take 500 units of Vitamin D every morning. It's necessary for calcium metabolism. You may be deficient. It can do you no harm, and may prevent another stone from forming."

I phoned for Corky to come and pick me up, walked out into the evening sunshine, and sat on a stone by the driveway. It seemed an incredibly long time since the night before—more like a month than a day.

I continued to have attacks of renal colic for another ten days or so. I absolutely hated the Demerol, but I took it as instructed. The stuff certainly deadened the pain, but it deadened everything else as well, knocked me into a stupid state like I'd been clobbered. I couldn't imagine anyone taking this garbage for kicks, but some people certainly did.

Eventually I passed the stone as expected. No great pain was involved as it made its way down the urethra into the handkerchief. Meanwhile I was drinking at least three mugs of tea for breakfast every day, and taking the Vitamin D. I have taken it every day since (along with the tea) and have had no recurrence of kidney stone. I don't drink as much as I should, perhaps, but I manage to get three litres or so into me daily. I never seem to feel thirsty, and that's perhaps a misfortune, perhaps the cause of the attack in the first place.

Meanwhile, I was working not only on the piece about the Saint John River, but on three other essays all for the same book: one on each of the two national parks in Newfoundland and one on the upper Churchill River in Saskatchewan. Fortunately, I already had all the needed information on those places, and did not need to visit them again. The fees for the four pieces and a magazine article on the Saint John kept me solvent in a year when my book royalties were not very large, and my expenses were soaring. Things looked a bit tight, at times, but I always managed to keep ahead of the bills.

My first project, after buying the house, was to pay off the mortgage. This took three years. Next was to continue adding space, in addition to the workroom—first of all, a garage for the car at street level on the highroad. You couldn't trust a car outside in the winter; it could be demolished or ploughed into oblivion. You could get to the highway on foot, even when the driveway was sheathed in solid ice. We levelled a site, poured concrete, and reinforced it with scrap steel that Mary Jane had salvaged. The path from the house to the garage was so steep that we added flights of wooden steps in two places.

My next project was a working cabin—a detached studio. At first I had tried to make the large bedroom where Corky and I and Andrew slept do double duty as a work room, but it was too close to the living room and kitchen where there was always a lot of noisy activity. So about a hundred yards from the house in deep woods we started a big one-room cabin. Its single attractive feature was a large triple window facing Beachy Cove Mountain. This window, another of Mary Jane's salvagings, has a tall centre pane with a rounded top, and two lower lights at the sides, an arrangement that reminded me of a church. There was a marvelous view, and it was in this cabin, looking through the window, that I wrote the seventeen-syllable haiku that became the opening sentence of my third novel: "I sit in a cabin surrounded by snow, remembering summer."

In that cabin I wrote *Beyond the Road* and most of the stories in *Only the Gods Speak*, as well as the crucial tenth version of my third novel. In it Andrew learned his letters, and read his first words from word-blocks that I made for him.

Let me explain. The blocks were wooden, about an inch and a half long, with hand-lettered cards glued to them—between seventy and eighty in all—short, common words that could be arranged in simple sentences. I knew, by now, that Andrew was dyslexic. As it turned out, he was severely dyslexic, but he worked at learning to read with dogged patience. It took fifteen years, but he did it, and eventually became an avid reader, going through stacks of books and such magazines as *Scientific American* and *National Geographic*. I consider his education an enormous triumph—first of all for him, secondly for the special education teachers who tutored him for eight years, and finally for me, who taught him everything past the grade nine level.

From the earliest age there were signs that Andrew was going to have perceptual problems. He was an unusually bright child, began talking very early, forming sentences before the age of two—but he used some very odd pronunciations. Distortions are normal for young children, of course, but extreme distortions like some of those used by Andrew often indicate trouble ahead. Far more revealing was his complete failure to crawl. He was physically strong, could walk, holding on, while still a small baby, but refused to crawl. If you put him on the floor he'd wiggle like a worm, but never went on hands and knees. He walked before he crawled. A knowledgeable visitor told us that babies who walked before they crawled usually had perceptual problems later. We dismissed this, but the perceptual problems appeared as soon as he tried to read.

Andrew was always strongly right-handed. This, together with his superior intelligence, and the effort he put into learning to read a few words long before "school age" disguised the dyslexia so that his early teachers, and even a professional "tester," missed that problem altogether, and thought they were dealing with an emotionally disturbed child rather than one with a perceptual disability. The dyslexia was only *professionally* diagnosed when I took him to the psychology lab at the University of Waterloo at the age of eight, where it showed up plainly enough in the analysis of brain-wave patterns. This analysis merely confirmed what I had known for six years, but his teachers found it convincing.

Emotionally, Andrew was stable, self-possessed, and even self-confident, the result of living in a family that understood his problem from the beginning, and tried to compensate. For the first seven or eight years of his life his mother spent hours reading to him every day. In fact he acquired, partly through such reading, and partly from the conversation that went on around him, a level of education far beyond his years, and was treated by his classmates, wherever he went to school, as a sort of walking encyclopaedia. Whenever they needed information, someone simply said, "Ask Andrew." He could never do much in a regular classroom. All but three of his eleven years of schooling were spent in classes especially organized to teach dyslexics. He was happy and successful in those classes, and was always popular with his classmates and teachers.

When I no longer needed it for work space, the cabin continued to be useful. For a while it was home to Harold Heap and Hilary Dixon, two members of the tribe who had arrived from Toronto in 1970, and who continued to live in the Newfoundland woods for twenty-two years. Harold was the son of Dan Heap, later an MP from downtown Toronto, where he won a seat for the NDP in a surprising upset. Hilary's father was in business, with an expensive house in a Toronto suburb. From Beachy Cove, Hilary and Harold moved to Jamestown, Bonavista Bay, built their own house and raised four children. They shared a patch of ground with Corky's daughter Ellie, and her man Frank and her son Jesse in a truly primitive place where moose wandered through the gardens and browsed from brush piles beside the door.

After Harold and Hilary moved out, the cabin was taken over by another wandering refugee from the sixties, Bob Allison, who raised his son Robin in that place until Robin left to spend a year travelling about Europe, and subsequently went off to British Columbia.

Tim, John and Des Walsh did most of the work on the cabin and the garage. Later, they worked on an attached greenhouse that I added to the south side of the house, and on a small detached greenhouse where we raised tomatoes and a few other plants.

You couldn't do much gardening there. It was all rocks. The house had been built for the view, with a commanding vista of Beachy Cove Valley and Conception Bay. Unfortunately the view was off to the north, and its great banks of double-glazed windows faced north, into the view, instead of south, into the sun. The attached greenhouse was an attempt to remedy this, at least in part—not entirely successful because the house was on a north-facing slope, with both land and trees rising to cut off the sunlight. The design of the house was excellent. If it could have been lifted off its concrete pad, turned around to face south, and set down on the top of the ridge, it would have been an excellent place to live. But its situation was appalling, on a rock above a valley, with driveway and paths that turned into frozen waterfalls for several months a year. Before I had spent three years there I began casting about for a more suitable place, one with a less mountainous approach, more exposure to the sun and some soil for gardening.

Except for the lack of soil, it was a great place in summer. Visitors were invariably impressed. Farley and Claire Mowat, Max Braithwaite, Margaret Laurence, Silver Donald Cameron, John David Hamilton (to mention only mainland writers) and the committee from the Canada Council all stood and goggled at the view.

Margaret spent a week with us on her only visit to Newfoundland, and was impressed as much by the dinners as by the view. She had no gifts for cooking, herself, but at Beachy Cove was surrounded by people who regarded food as one of the fine arts. John, Dennie and I all competed for the right to make dinner, doing our favourite dishes. John was expert at that English tradition, roast beef and Yorkshire pudding. Dennie liked to make such Italian things as lasagne. I did Chinese cooking, stir-fried foods and things with sweet and sour sauces.

One of the things I remember from the visit of the Canada Council panel is that all those mainlanders ate seal flippers for the first time in their lives and licked their chops as they washed them down with Burgundy (It should have been Screech, I suppose, but there are limits, even to being a Newfie among mainlanders). We also fed them on clam chowder with onions, peppers and thyme, thickened, as it should be, with shaved potatoes.

The financial strain of taking on that large family in that large house, entertaining streams of visitors and trying to make the place more livable was all rather daunting. The $24,000 I'd had when I moved in didn't last very long. My capital outlay was just over $40,000 in four years, so besides meeting current expenses I had to find an additional $16,000.

I did what writers usually do in such circumstances—I applied for a senior arts grant from the Canada Council. My luck was in, and I got the grant for the purpose of completing *Remembering Summer* and my short story collection *Only the Gods Speak*. This should have put me back in business, for senior arts awards were then worth $12,000. But there was a catch. That year, for the first and only time, the Canada Council decided to stay within its budget by cutting all its arts awards in half. So I and other senior writers got $6,000 each.

The Council helped out in other ways, though. I sat on a number of juries, thankfully pocketing the fees and the travelling expenses. For a year I was a member of the Arts Advisory Panel and the Task Force on Policy. It all added up to another three or four thousand dollars in revenue.

At that period, too, Paperjacks decided to issue three of my books in mass-market format. Two of them, *White Eskimo* and *The Foxes of Beachy Cove*, became national best sellers. Since I didn't have a money-making new book ready for publication between 1972 and 1976, those varied sources of income were life-savers. It was a time when I could easily have sunk out of sight, when I could have been forced back into full-time journalism. What little journalism I did was exclusively on commission—mainly for *Reader's Digest* and for *International Wildlife*. I averaged a badly needed $6,000 a year from this source, and did it with very little time and effort, because I always worked from minimum research. I rarely spent more than six or seven days on a magazine article, and could usually do the final edit and rewrite in a few hours. Sometimes I could do all the interviews by telephone without leaving the house. In effect, this kind of journalism provided me with an income supplement of $6,000 to $8,000 a year without cutting into my time as a creative writer.

Chapter 12

In 1975, Andrew was a year old, running around and talking. Jonathan was eleven, played with the baby a lot, and gave him some of the toys that he was outgrowing—metal cars and trucks and tractors. He played with them endlessly. "Better he should be crazy about cars now than when he's eighteen," Leslie remarked. Among our keepsake photographs there is a rather funny one of Andrew at that age feeding Jonathan a cracker.

In early autumn Ellie went off to Ontario, then to Minnesota to visit Corky's sister, then back to Ontario, where she gave birth to her son Jesse in a hippie house in Mississauga, with two untrained women as birth attendants. According to her own story, they gave her some kind of herbal tea to drink and chanted mantras. Otherwise, nature took its course, and the baby was born healthy. Rozie had gone to Mississauga to be with her sister. I was in Toronto without a car (having driven to a union meeting in Ottawa with my neighbour, the novelist Bill Percy). So I shopped around for a used car to take Ellie, Rozie, the baby and myself back home. I found an Austin America 1970 seemingly in beautiful shape for $650, and started home on November 14. We were within 35 miles of North Sydney when the car blew its engine. We left it on the shoulder in a pool of oil, and got a cab to the Newfoundland ferry. From the terminal I phoned the RCMP, asked them to have the car towed to a garage, and gave them my address. I meant to ship it to St. John's and there install a rebuilt engine. The body and interior appeared to be in showroom condition. That was the last I ever heard of the car. The police did not get in touch with me. When I tried to talk with *them*, I learned that the man I'd been talking to at Baddeck had been transferred. They had no information about the car. Short of making a trip to Baddeck and going the rounds of the garages, I seemed to be out of luck. By now it was winter. I simply wrote off the car, and forgot it.

In the summer of 1975 1 had two national bestsellers in Paperjacks: *White Eskimo* and *The Foxes of Beachy Cove*. *Tomorrow Will Be Sunday* was also in its second or third paperback reprint. *Beyond the Road* was on press with Van Nostrand Reinhold. I flew to Montreal at *Reader's Digest's* expense, and from there continued as a guest of the native leaders to do research and write a report on the final stages of the James Bay development, which was then close to a settlement. Back at Beachy Cove, John and I, with help from Jonathan, finished building a seaworthy sixteen-foot boat for use on Conception Bay. I used plans supplied by the College of Trades and Technology for the use of fishermen. The boat was excellent, but we used it only a few times before it was wrecked in an unexpected summer gale at Portugal Cove.

I was invited, in August, to go to the University of British Columbia to take part in weekend readings by six Canadian fiction writers—Graeme Gibson, Margaret Atwood and I from what British Columbians regard as the East Coast, Bob Kroetsch from the Prairies, Andreas Schroeder and Audrey Thomas from the Pacific Coast. The readings would be in mid-September, so Corky and I decided to take the proffered airfare and drive to Vancouver in my Honda Civic, camping by a northern route on the way out, and a southern one coming home.

She and I and Andrew left Toronto on September 4 for a motor trip that we estimated would be about 10,000 miles. We crossed at Sault Ste. Marie, and drove to Pequot Lakes in southern Minnesota to visit Corky's sister Vicki and her husband

Doug Hanson. We then drove westward through the Dakotas, and into southern Saskatchewan through a marvellous stretch of the Badlands. We camped in the Rocky Mountains in temperatures well below freezing, then headed down the Icefields Parkway through some of the most spectacular landscape on the continent, and arrived at Penticton on September 12, where it was still midsummer, and we went swimming. We were swimming again next day in the Pacific at Stanley Park, and then crossed from Horseshoe Bay for a tour of Vancouver Island as far as Campbell River and Kelsey Bay. On the island we practically lived on free oysters, which we collected from public beaches. By the afternoon of September 19 we were back in Vancouver for the "weekend with Canadian novelists."

The evening that I was to read, I discovered that I had arrived at the university auditorium without a book or a page of manuscript in my briefcase. I dashed back to the hotel, grabbed the manuscript of the short story, "The Sound of Thunder," and a chunk of my novel-in- process *Remembering Summer*, and got back in time to be introduced to the audience.

I read the short story and got a round of applause. Then I explained that I had a section of an autobiographical novel on which I was working, and plunged straight into it. In the middle of reading the chapter I'd picked out I suddenly discovered that this was where I went into the intensely personal exploration of how Eli meets and falls in love with Dannie—how sex ceased to matter, etc. etc. I was appalled. Suddenly here I was, quite unintentionally being as exhibitionistic as hell in front of an audience of hundreds of teachers and writers. There was nothing to do but continue. The audience, however, was grabbed. There was a silence that suggested they were holding their breath—and then, when I'd finished, the kind of applause that could only be called an ovation. Someone talked about "a new departure in Canada in confessional literature," but that was just an anticlimax. It was one of the most memorable points in my career—the other being twelve years later, when I visited Chautauqua with *Dancing on the Shore.*

We headed south for the Oregon coast. Andrew was now sixteen months old, on his first long trip by car, and though it was a great experience for him he was, to say the least, a trial. At times I pulled off the road and announced that I wasn't going any further until he shut up. We camped on beaches covered with driftwood along a shoreline that was overpowering in its immensity. A few refugees from the sixties were still to be found travelling around the country in those days. On one beach we had for next door neighbour a young man travelling without a tent, but with what he regarded as the real necessities—a sleeping bag, a stocking cap, a frisbee, and a copy of *Rolling Stone.* He had arrived on the west coast from Michigan with no more equipment than he could carry in one hand.

On September 25 we camped under a redwood that measured fifteen feet across the butt, centre of a clump some twenty-five feet in diameter. Later that day we drove into Sacramento, where the temperature was 100°F in the shade, then up into the Carson Range of the Sierras to 7,000 feet, where we camped beside a mountain torrent among huge granite boulders. Next day we drove to an elevation of more than 10,000 feet, and saw the 4,000-year-old bristlecone pines. For the first time, I was bothered a bit by the altitude, though I'd felt just great at 9,000 feet in Mexico. We drove across the valley and camped on the slope of Mount Whitney, the highest peak in the Sierras. Next day we visited Mono Lake, where pillars of alkaline salts stand about in the image of Lot's wife, and the water tastes poisonous to humans, though masses of migrating shorebirds make use of it. Then we drove across Death Valley, where the temperature was 112°F in the shade, and went swimming at Lake Mead above Boulder Dam. Near here, standing just off the highroad, we saw a magnificent Rocky Mountain bighorn sheep with a huge set of crescent horns.

We passed through handsome stands of cactus in Arizona, and saw both the Grand Canyon and the Painted Desert before arriving at Blue Lake, New Mexico, just east of the continental divide on September 28. There we went swimming again, while Andrew floated about on an air mattress. By October 2 we were in northern Mississippi. From there we headed northward through Tennessee to Bowling Green, Kentucky, where we visited Louise Travelsted, who had spent a sabbatical year teaching in Labrador in 1950, and whom I had visited several times before, both in Bowling Green and in New York City, where she had a penthouse apartment overlooking Fifth Avenue.

We then continued northward through beautiful autumn weather in Kentucky and Ohio, and crossed into Canada on October 6. There we camped on the shore of Lake Erie, went swimming, ate steak and chips cooked on our camp stove, and celebrated with rum and cola beside a huge fire of driftwood.

Next we visited Edna Staebler at Sunfish Lake, near Waterloo, and stayed for several days. I did a public reading at the Kitchener-Waterloo library, then spent several days in Toronto before heading back to Newfoundland. When we arrived at Beachy Cove we had been away nearly two months, and to Andrew the trip must have seemed to go on almost forever. As we drove through St. Phillip's I told him, "In a few minutes we are going to see Rozie and Dennie and John, and Eric the dog." He thought about this, round-eyed. Like returning to a former lifetime.

That was not my first trip by car across North America, but it was the first of many trips that Corky and I made together to all parts of the continent between Newfoundland, Vancouver Island, the Blue Ridge Mountains, the cypress swamps of the

Gulf of Mexico, the barrier islands of the American east coast, and the dry uplands of Florida. But for me it was not the end of travelling, even for that year. On October 26 I was in Ottawa, on October 29 at Half Moon Bay on the coast of British Columbia, doing research for yet another magazine article, and on November 2 I was at Great Rideau Lake, Ontario, having a birthday dinner with the Buck family, and with Carol and Bernard Desoeur, both of whose birthdays, like mine, fall on November 2. That same evening I went on to Montreal and then to Halifax, had late supper at a restaurant at 1:30 A.M., fell into a hotel bed, and arrived back at Torbay airport at 11:45 the same morning. I still have the expense account I submitted for that trip. Back and forth across the continent with stopovers in about six places, cabs, car rentals, hotels, telephone tolls—the whole thing came to a mere $832.93—almost unbelievable today.

By the summer of 1976 the pressures on me were not quite so great. John, Tim, and Des were all drawing unemployment insurance as a result of work they'd done for me. Jonathan was now twelve years old, and his family's crisis was past. Then a number of lucky breaks came my way in quick succession.

The University of Victoria offered me a teaching post in their creative writing department. I think they had one visiting teacher each year. Before I actually got around to accepting it I had a phone call from the University of Western Ontario offering me a residency. This happened to be a much better offer, as I'd be expected to be on campus only half-time between September 15 and April 15. The salary was $16,000, and there would certainly be reading fees and other fringe benefits. Jack McClelland asked me to do a book for a history of Canada that he was planning to publish in some fifteen volumes. He was paying $8,000 for each book, without royalties. I said I'd like to do the period between the Cabot voyages and the fall of New France.

His editors were delighted; no other writer had expressed an interest in the early colonial era. I was interested in it because Newfoundland history was so prominent a part of it, and because Canadians other than Newfoundlanders were not even aware that Newfoundland had any history, much less that it had been so important in the sixteenth to the eighteenth centuries.

As it turned out, the residency at the University of Western Ontario combined beautifully with the books I was writing—books that required a lot of research, which the university provided free of charge. I was within a few steps of the main research library, and not only could get access to printouts of all documents I needed, but also to copies, in the rare book room, of all needed materials from New France. Research I had already done for a radio series on the French in Newfoundland supplemented Prowse's *History*, Lescarbot's *New France*, Champlain's *Journals*, and Mother Marie's *Letters*. The editors told me later that mine was the best piece of social history in the series. At Western, too, I completed *Beyond The Road*, and worked on *Bartlett*, though I did not finish the latter until three years later, at Waterloo.

I worked hard at being a writer-in-residence, and established a high standard of usefulness to the university. I helped members of the faculty edit their manuscripts, showed students how to get their visions into imaginative prose or poetry, and made myself available to the public as well as to the university. People came from as far as Hamilton to see me. Other professional writers were at hand. James Reaney was on campus. So were Colleen Thibideau and Larry Garber. I had first met Garber at the founding of the Writers' Union. I had published some of Thibideau's early poetry in *Protocol* many years before. On Wednesdays, Alice Munro would come to town from the snowbound village where she lived, and she and Garber and I would have lunch together.

I tried to work up interest in founding a new literary journal, but failed to find much enthusiasm for it at London. The job remained to be accomplished at the University of Waterloo five years later.

Corky and I had decided that we didn't want to live in the city of London. By good fortune we managed to find a partially "winterized" summer cabin at Grand Bend on the shore of Lake Huron. The house wasn't anything to boast about, and it was forty miles from the campus, requiring a lot of commuting in my little Honda Civic, but it was amply worth the trouble. We had endless miles of beautiful sand beach, huge wooded dunes with red oaks and red pines, fascinating places to visit up and down the eastern shore of that splendid inland sea. We swam in surf until the last possible minute in October, sunbathed in the dunes, and in winter took Andrew tobogganing on the same slopes where we lay in the sun during autumn and spring. It was, in fact, a very happy year, with everything going right.

Corky was now pregnant again, and due to have her baby in December. We decided this time to dispense completely with doctors, hospitals, and the interventions of the medical people. She was forty-eight—the same age as her own mother when she was born, full of good health, in absolutely top shape, and quite convinced that nothing could go wrong.

"Women who worry about their pregnancies aren't properly in touch with their own bodies," she said. "Pregnancy isn't a disease. You can tell how a baby is doing. You can feel how it's getting on. If anything was even slightly wrong, I wouldn't need a medical examination to find out, I'd know."

So we never consulted a doctor before, during, or after Corky's last pregnancy. This time I was much less apprehensive than I had been at Andrew's birth. I now accepted birth as a natural event that required no intervention if things were normal, and by this time, at least, I knew exactly what was meant by "tying off" an umbilical cord—a matter that early editions of *Our Bodies, Ourselves* had neglected to deal with.

Corky was never even slightly ill, had no morning sickness, didn't look pregnant, and no one outside our immediate family suspected it. We didn't tell my parents, because we didn't want Vina trying to interfere, as she had done when Corky was pregnant with Andrew.

Around the first of December, less than a week before she was "due" according to the reckoning that doctors tell you to use (but not according to the reckoning that I had learned as a boy, which is nine months and ten days from the *date of conception*, regardless of the menstrual period) we drove to London and flew to St. John's for a brief visit. My parents still didn't suspect that Corky was nine months pregnant. John, Dennie, and the rest of them at Beachy Cove seemed to be coping well enough without our help. Rozie decided to go back with us to help out after the birth.

Ten days later we flew to Toronto and drove to Grand Bend. Corky was feeling just fine, the baby now supposedly "overdue." The unborn child was quite lively, and you could feel the head-down orientation. Corky had engaged in no kind of "preparation." She was opposed to the whole set of values that had led to North American obstetrics—to X-ray tests for this and that, drugged deliveries, induced labours, playpens and formulas, feeding schedules, generation gaps and the old folks' homes. Once you have decided on natural childbirth, the next step is to drop all the other nonsense along with the obstetrician.

We had agreed that there was to be no birth attendant other than myself and Andrew. What I would need to do would be absolutely minimal. The idea that you must "deliver" a baby is a misconception. Babies deliver themselves, helped along by a strong push from mother's trunk muscles. Doctors with forceps may be needed, on very rare occasions, but on occasion, too, they turn the child into a lifelong cripple.

Corky and I awakened around 3:00 A.M. on December 13, when the amniotic sac ruptured.

"It's started," she said.

We got up, put on the lights, and made some tea. Rozie and Andrew remained asleep. By 6:30 we had eaten breakfast, and Corky was walking about in a housecoat. She was having contractions, but they were not painful.

"I think I'll go take a shower," she said; then, a moment later, changed her mind: "No, I don't think there'll be time."

I had already replaced the sheets on our bed with a sheet of plastic. I had no idea how much, or little, mess there might be. I had seen calves born, but this was my first human. Corky went and lay on the bed. Andrew went into an adjoining room with Rozie. I put the breakfast dishes into the sink and started to wash them. A snowstorm was raging outside.

I was still doing the dishes when Corky called to me, "Better come in now." I dried my hands on the dish towel and went into the bedroom, where Corky was lying naked on the bed. She was not crouching. There's nothing wrong with a crouching birth, of course. It's just not the only way to do it. She was lying flat on her back, knees raised and spread. I had no time to take off my ring or my watch, or make any other preparation. The crown of the baby's head was already in sight. Corky made one last effort, and the head emerged. The baby began to breathe instantly, and made her first faint cry.

"Is it born?" Corky asked.

"Not quite. Just the head."

She pushed again, and I slipped my hands around the shoulders and pulled gently, and there she was, lying on the plastic.

"It's a girl," I said. "She's double-corded. It's wrapped around her neck twice." I picked up the cord.

"Don't stretch it," Corky said.

She sat up. We lifted the baby, and turned her twice to unwrap the umbilical cord. I laid her on her mother's belly, and Corky covered her with her hands.

Two-and-a-half-year-old Andrew had now appeared in the doorway.

"I heard a little cry, like a cat," he said.

"Yes. Come see."

He stood beside the bed while I explained why the baby was attached by a cord to her mother. The birth had not been messy. There was no fresh blood, just a very little dark, clotted stuff, and some scraps of whitish amniotic tissue.

"What time is it?" Corky asked.

"Twenty minutes after seven."

"You lose track of time while it's happening," she said. "You don't know whether it's minutes or hours."

I was worried because the baby looked purplish. Had being corded reduced her oxygen supply? Only later did I learn that it's the natural color at birth. Anyway, her color was obviously temporary, because the baby was slowly turning pink before my eyes. I went to the bathroom, and filled the sink with water at about blood heat.

By now the cord had collapsed, and I went for scissors and dental floss. I tied the floss with an ordinary square knot as close, to the baby's belly as I could, tied it again, a couple of inches away, and snipped the cord between. While tying the cord I could see that my hands were trembling—my first shot of adrenalin in a long time. I took the baby to the bathroom and lowered her into the warm water. At that point she yowled for the second time. She didn't want to be washed even in lukewarm water. I rinsed off the scraps of tissue as quickly as I could, dried her on a towel and held her against my left shoulder. She stopped crying and made sucking movements. I took her back to her mother, and she sucked until she went to sleep. Corky covered her with a blanket.

At this point the placenta still had not emerged, and I was a bit worried by the delay, though I'd seen it before in dairy cattle, and I suspected it wasn't important. Corky wasn't bleeding, so there was no reason to suspect anything wrong.

"Well, I'm tired of lying here," she said. "I'm going to the bathroom." She went and sat on the toilet, and a couple of minutes later I heard it flush.

"So much for that," she said. "The placenta has gone down the drain." Much later I heard that it is illegal, in Canada, to flush a placenta down the drain or put it in the garbage. You are supposed to save it and bury it (I suppose in consecrated ground, though I'm not sure about that detail. Many carnivorous animals eat it, and it is doubtless very nutritious). Anyway, down the drain it went, and good riddance.

Other oddities about the law of birth in Canada, or anyway in Ontario, soon appeared. I went to the town hall to register the birth.

"Oh, the doctor does that," the clerk told me.

"There was no doctor. The baby was born at home."

"Here? In Grand Bend?"

"Of course. This is where we live."

It took them a long time to locate the forms, because no baby had been born in Grand Bend during the past fifteen years. Eventually some old yellowed ones turned up in a safe. I filled them in and mailed them off to the county seat. They came back with a letter explaining that the law had been changed. You now had to register all births at Queen's Park in Toronto, and on new forms of a more modern design.

I wrote for the redesigned forms, and they came, in duplicate, one for a parent (either parent for a wonder) and one for the attending physician. I filled out the form for the parent and sent it off to the bureaucrats, explaining that there was no attending physician. My form came back. The law required a form from the attending physician, so I must fill out the forms twice, and sign them twice, once as a parent, and once as the attending physician. I suppose a woman giving birth alone would be her own attending physician in the eyes of the bureaucrats.

At about 10:00 A.M. on December 13 I phoned my father, told him that we'd just had our second baby, and that she was named Leah. He was astonished, but pleased that we had named the baby after his own mother—the first of her scores of grandchildren and great-grandchildren that had been so named.

A family doctor told me, many years ago, "The only disinfectant you should have in your house is soap and water. Anything stronger will just do harm, perhaps by destroying symbiotic bacteria on your skin—the bacteria that help defend you against invasion. Destroy them with disinfectants and you open yourself to the first skin-burrowing organism that comes along."

Neither Corky nor Leah was disinfected, before or after birth. The baby was born in the midst of pubic hair that had not been shaved or even washed. She lay on her mother's unwashed belly for several minutes while the cord collapsed. It should, of course, not be tied or cut until it ceases to function. This is so obvious that it is hard to believe people have to be told about it, hard to believe that even hospital people, with their impatience, their training to look on life as mechanistic, could have fallen into the habit of cutting off the umbilical flow artificially the moment the baby was out of the birth canal—and incidentally spilling a few squirts of blood in the process.

During her first ten years of life Leah never saw a doctor except, perhaps, on the street. The only nurse she saw professionally was the one who gave her immunizing shots in a clinic. At the age of twelve she broke an arm in a sledding accident and needed medical treatment for the first time. Except for a slight cold now and then she was never sick.

When Corky reached her fiftieth birthday she was still breastfeeding this child. Like her brother, Leah was fed on human milk almost exclusively for the first year, and continued to nurse until well past the age of two. She never tasted baby food or "formula" or any such artificial junk. When she began to taste solid food she had mashed banana. When she ceased nursing, she drank cow's milk from a cup. Neither of our children ever sucked from a bottle (or from a thumb, either).

Leah and Andrew knew nothing about sibling rivalry. They were each other's best friends from the time she was born until well after she went to school. Even when they were teenagers and being educated in separate towns, they couldn't wait to get together and share their time on weekends. They squabbled and teased, but never fought or really quarreled, never competed for their parents' attentions, or were jealous of each other's achievements or possessions. Everything he learned he passed on to her as quickly as he could. By the age of three she could distinguish the common poisonous mushrooms from the ones Andrew picked for the table, and tell whether an evergreen tree was a spruce or a fir. They had almost no sense of possessionship. The day after we gave her a new tricycle for her fourth birthday she explained to me that it wasn't really a tricycle—it was Andrew's Model-T car. When we gave him his first bicycle, it was she who rode it, while he rode an old one on loan from a neighbour.

Of course there were problems—they just weren't the kind of problems that the prevailing North American culture inflicts on the North American family. Our children never refused to eat because they were never urged to do so, never became addicted to junk food because it was never offered to them, never ran to fat, never wished to have money or trendy clothes or a lot of the garbage they saw advertised on TV, never were the least bit afraid of the dark, never listened to loud pop music, and never regarded their parents as doddering old fools. They always got along well with classmates and teachers, but most of all they seemed to enjoy the company of visiting adults. They had friends of their own age, occasionally fairly close friends, but in general they preferred to talk with people who knew enough about the world and its surroundings to be able to talk intelligently. By the time they were in their early teens our visitors were regularly astonished at the level of their knowledge.

How do you accomplish all this? Simple. You do it by not trying. If you're lucky, you have read the Taoist sages, and have tried to govern your life accordingly. Especially, you stop trying so hard to bend the world to your own will. You go with the flow, turn your back to the wind, trust life's unfolding. When you do that, most difficulties disappear.

Chapter 13

In the spring of 1977, while I was writer-in-residence at the University of Western Ontario, I was invited to do readings at high schools and libraries in various parts of the province. The students, mostly in grade eleven and twelve, proved to be really great audiences with whom I could discuss anything from the sexual revolution (a great theme in those days) to the cultural disaster created in the classical world by the spread of the Christian superstition.

But I almost came to grief at the town of Renfrew, about fifty miles west of Ottawa, where a school had requested three Canadian writers for a morning of readings. Sylvia Fraser, who had recently published *The Candy Factory* ("takes up where *Fear of Flying* left off"), Don Bailey (*In the Belly of the Whale*, all about serving time for armed robbery) and I were invited to the school together at the suggestion of the union touring office. What the office hadn't told us was that it was a junior high-school, where we'd be meeting twelve- and thirteen-year-old kids.

Things began to go wrong when the school principal drove out to the little local airport the evening before the readings to pick up Don Bailey. As they approached Renfrew, Don remarked, "I remember this place. I robbed a bank here once."

"At that point the poor guy barely escaped driving into the ditch," he told me.

The three of us had arrived with our usual supplies of sex, drugs and violence. The principal hurried off to the librarian to check on our antecedents. When he discovered that he had a bank robber, a writer on kinky sex, and a retailer of drug visions on his hands he was as appalled as the three writers were to find themselves facing an audience so recently out of diapers. Next morning he sent us a very nervous note saying that every writer must have written some things suitable for school children, and could we please bear in mind that our innocent audience would be expecting innocent prose.

Somehow we muddled through. I don't know how Don and Sylvia managed, because we spoke simultaneously to separate sections of the school, but I heard that they went over extremely well indeed. As for me, having brought nothing with me except the manuscript of *Remembering Summer* and my short story *The Sound of Thunder* (both *very* adult fiction indeed), I was reduced to spinning an impromptu story about living beside the sea, beachcombing, the noctiluca lighting up the waves, leading on to the food chain at the sea's edge. I was just into the meat of what I hoped was an entertaining biology lesson when the librarian arrived with a copy of *The Foxes of Beachy Cove*, and all thenceforth was sweetness and light. The principal saved his job, and the union's touring office learned to be more careful about matching readers to audiences.

Shortly thereafter Corky and the kids and I headed back to Beachy Cove. On our way through St. Jean Port Joli, Quebec, we went down to the beach to see the mobs of snow geese that stop off there each spring on their way to nesting grounds on Baffin Island—surely one of the great sights for anyone interested in birds. Almost the entire world population of lesser snow geese concentrates on a short stretch of the St. Lawrence shore every spring to rest and feed before undertaking the last leg of their great northward journey. Consequently they are in grave danger from an oil spill should there be a major one in the St. Lawrence River. There may be other dangers, from the same pollution that is killing off the beluga whales, for instance. One way or another, we could be the last generation to witness the great flocks of migrating snow geese along the Atlantic flyway.

We arrived back at Beachy Cove on May 8, and I found myself in a very "down" mood. Not only was Andrew suffering from bronchitis and an ear infection, but the place was beginning to depress me, as it never had when I lived up on the ridge. The four acres of land on which Corky's house stood were not only rocky, but also a mess of cutover and blowdown, with fir regrowing in spindly thickets almost as dense as grass in a field. I tried clearing out patches, but the work didn't go well.

Things improved in July when Jack Hermann, the potter, arrived from Ontario determined to "do" Newfoundland, and we took him on a tour of the south coast. We travelled by coastal ship from Argentia to Port aux Basques, and by great good luck enjoyed fine weather, so that we actually got to see such places as Paradise Sound and Petit Forte, Mortier Bay, Bay d'Espoir, Grey River and the Ramea Islands. Most of those places I knew already, but to Corky and Jack the voyage had a kind of magic quality. Leah was too young to remember any of it, but to Andrew it was another experience that helped set him up for life as an eager traveller. Jack returned from Port aux Basques to the mainland, but Corky and I and the kids made the return trip by coastal vessel, and loved every minute of it.

In late July, back at Beachy Cove, I cleared a piece of land on one of the thickest patches of second growth, not far from the cabin. There I spent many days of late summer reading and sunbathing in the nude. I planned to use the ground, which was protected from the wind and had a southerly slope, to grow potatoes the following year, for it seemed reasonably fertile. It was one of those rare, beautiful summers when the climate of eastern Newfoundland is nearly perfect. What little ground we did have produced lots of vegetables, and there was an enormous harvest of wild fruit. In early September I spent six or seven days on the barrens near Mount Pearl, shirtless and barefooted in bright sunshine and crystal air, picking twenty-five gallons of blueberries and seven gallons of raspberries. All told that year we had more than forty gallons of wild berries.

The Bartlett biography came out on November 4 (much too late for a buildup to Christmas sales) and I had to do a mad scramble of a tour through Ontario, Quebec, and the Atlantic Provinces. I was particularly well received in Nova Scotia and Newfoundland, but mainlanders showed little interest in "the greatest ice captain of modern times" as Rasmussen called him. This was one more instance of the parochialism of central Canadians. Half the population of the country lives in Ontario. Half the remainder lives in Quebec. Few of those have any interest in Canada's three great coastal regions. They think rural Canada means living down on the farm. Nevertheless, Doubleday, to their credit, have kept this book in print for more than twenty years. Bartlett was a far more admirable person than Abram Kean, but a more difficult subject for the biographer. There was one great drama in Kean's life, perfectly shaped for a book like *Death on the Ice*. Bartlett's career, after the *Karluk* adventure, was a long story of anticlimax, spread over the following thirty years—not the liveliest material for a "page-turner"—but he was unquestionably the Newfoundland seafarer most deserving a serious biography.

Corky and I went touring around Nova Scotia off and on for two years before we settled, tentatively, on the Annapolis Valley as the most likely place to build our next house. It had the best all-round climate in the Atlantic Provinces, the lowest snowfall of any part of Nova Scotia; it had excellent soil; the area that interested us was also close to the Bay of Fundy car ferry, which in turn would put me within easy driving of Montreal, or even make it possible to reach Toronto in one long day's drive. This would be quite a change from Beachy Cove, which was three days, by surface travel, from just about anywhere else.

In December I joined the Arts Advisory Panel of the Canada Council, and served on my first Canada Council jury. To get to a meeting in Ottawa that winter I would get up at 4:00 A.M., make my way in darkness over the ice falls to the highroad, get my car out of the garage, and drive to the airport. The early flight from Torbay stopped at Halifax, then went on to Ottawa, and arrived around 9:00 A.M., so I could be in time for the meeting without adding an extra day's travel, but it was rough going.

The Arts Advisory Panel was doing interesting work, reviewing policy on grants and other arts funding, and while I was there we set up the task force on the future of the Canada Council itself. After many meetings, Roch Carrier produced a first draft, in French, of our recommendations, and I helped translate it into English. Proposing general policies for the Council's next twenty-five years, it was published in both languages, and had an instant effect on both policy and morale inside the Council which, as usual, was under fire from the more reactionary members of the House of Commons, and in need of moral support from all parts of the cultural industry.

Des Walsh moved in with us that winter, staying in a spare bedroom that I had just finished. He was working on his second book of poetry, and playing with a musical group in St. John's nightclubs. He was also working as an editor with Breakwater Books, who had now accepted my collection of short stories, *Only the Gods Speak*, though the book didn't actually appear until the autumn of 1979.

In the spring of 1978, Corky, Andrew, Leah and I left on a month-long camping trip, travelling in the Honda and living in a tent. We camped at Great Rideau Lake near Ottawa in time for the great soaring flight of the Canada geese, at Pinery Provincial Park on the shore of Lake Huron, where Andrew got to revisit scenes he recalled from his third year, in the mountains of New England, and finally on the shore of Annapolis Basin.

We arrived at Smith's Cove near Digby in early May, and camped there when the chuckly pears (service berries) were in bloom, and the woods on all sides were great drifts of pink and white blossoms. I cannot believe that the cherry blossoms in Housman's England are in any way superior to the chuckly pears of the Annapolis Valley. If anything were needed to clinch our decision to live there, the sea of spring blossoms would have done it. We drove to the real-estate office in Annapolis Royal, and bought the piece of land where we would later build our house.

It was just a hayfield, with a patch of white and yellow birch growing in one corner near the highway, and three or four acres of scrub growth that we would later develop into a woodlot. But it had great possibilities: a beach fronting on the salt water of the Annapolis Basin, a clam flat, a bit of bog with a few cranberries, a few peach trees, a fine ridge some fifty feet above the beach where a house could be built overlooking the Basin, and a long ravine winding through the scrub trees, with sites to which we could divert a small stream and build two or three ponds.

The money to buy the land ($16,500) came from the sale of a first collection of my working papers and letters to the library of the University of Calgary, and from a little money we'd saved during our year at Grand Bend. After buying the land, we still had enough to begin building a house, with the help of loans from relatives, friends, and the bank. We secured demand loans, and never did take out a mortgage. The most generous help I received was from Farley and Claire Mowat, who loaned us $10,000 (which I repaid within three years) and made us an outright gift of another $10,000—one of many examples of Farley's exceptional generosity.

We had small monthly payments coming from Beachy Cove, where John and Dennie and Rozie were buying my share of the house on a thirteen-year payment plan. (We gave them Corky's share as a gift). A few years later I was able to help my nephew Charles acquire his first house, then to finance a house for my niece Janet and her husband Jamie, and—all within a couple of years—to finance houses for Corky's daughters Della and Rozie. So all-told I've been involved in financing six houses all without mortgages. I was fortunate to get into the buying and selling of securities, mostly through a broker, during the great bull market of the 1980s and '90s, and discovered, much to my own and everyone else's surprise, that I was able to make money in dividends, interest, and capital gains.

In the spring of '78 there were thirteen people living in our house at Beachy Cove. Besides Corky and me and the two children, there were Ellie and Jesse, John, Dennie, Rozie, Tim and Della (all of Corky's first family except for Michael, who had never moved to Newfoundland). Then there was Hilary Dixon, one of the refugees from Toronto, and Sid Maunder, a former classmate of John's, who had simply moved in and stayed. A few years later he moved, with Della and their two sons, to British Columbia.

In August we packed the car and the tent and went to Upper Clements. We lived in the tent beside the beach (a place that has been a campsite ever since) and there we canned our first crop of peaches, using a Coleman stove and sealers we had brought with us. While living in the tent we built a garage near the railway track at the front of our land. The materials cost us $360, Corky and I doing the work ourselves. We installed a wood stove and moved into the garage, the four of us sleeping on a wide bench, rather in the fashion of an Inuit igloo. We then began clearing brush and planting trees. I had learned from my first place at Beachy Cove that tree planting is the very first thing you should do on a piece of land where you plan to live.

Meanwhile, my nephew Charles had built himself a very small cabin in which to live while he put in the foundation of our house. The Hall brothers of Deep Brook, just south of our place, did the excavation, located a well site with the help of a divining rod, dug an excellent shallow well with a backhoe, and scooped a place in the ravine for a brook to form the first of our ponds.

We planted only fifty-nine trees that autumn—oak, maple, larch, spruce, and a couple of white pines. Then I left for St. John's, while Corky, the kids and Charles remained at Upper Clements. I had to leave the car at St. John's for an engine overhaul while I returned to Upper Clements early in October to find Charles taking down the forms from the foundation. He then put in sills for the ground floor, and covered it with rough board, storing wood in the basement to dry a little over winter. On October 20 I left by ferry and train for Canada Council meetings in Ottawa, then flew to Halifax, and hitched a ride from Halifax to Upper Clements in the middle of the night, arriving at 4:30 A.M., October 25. We continued to work at the house until early December, then headed back to Beachy Cove for Christmas and the winter.

Late in March 1979 we left for Upper Clements again, arriving on April 1, and moved back into the garage. Charles was now putting up the framing of the house, and rushing to get it covered, so we could camp inside while we worked to make it permanently habitable. I took the back seat out of the Honda Civic, converting the little car into a very small truck, and hauled all the building materials from the mills and the hardware stores. By the end of summer the wiring, the plumbing, the windows and the doors were all in place, the roof was covered, cedar siding was on, and Corky and I were working to install insulation and to cover the inside ceilings and walls. It was beautiful, an impressive house, on which we did all the inside work ourselves, with occasional help from Ellie and Charles. The total cost, including the land, was $50,009.87, but this did not include the two attached greenhouses which were part of the original plan, and which we added in subsequent years. Creating such a house at such a modest cost was, I felt, a major achievement.

We had decided to sell the house at Beachy Cove to John, Dennie and Rozie for the amount of money that I had actually put into the place, to be paid in monthly installments over a period of thirteen years, interest-free. Their payments amounted to $360 a month, which they felt they could manage, and though the work they did at St. John's was mostly casual and intermittent, they did manage it, and were never more than a month late with any of their payments. For a bunch of hippies left over from the sixties, they weren't doing too badly at all.

That year the Writers' Union was in dire trouble. It was the year of the "dues crisis" when we almost ran on the rocks. June Callwood was elected to the chair at the convention in May, and because the union was now falling to pieces, I put my name forward for the First vice-chair, determined to use every effort to pull it together again. June, who kept her head remarkably well through the union's darkest hour, consulted me by phone almost every week, and we met frequently in Toronto. But if I was going to take the chair the following year, I was going to have to be there almost full-time. So one of June's jobs was to try to find some kind of appointment (a university residency or temporary teaching post) that would enable me to live within commuting distance of Toronto the following year, leading up to the ninth annual meeting in the spring of 1981.

The best possibility seemed to be Trent University at Peterborough, where Margaret Laurence had been writer-in-residence, and where certain members of the faculty had already asked me if I would be interested. The problem there was money. They seemed to have only about half the financing needed to pay the university's share of a residency for 1980-81. They wrote and told me they were working on it, that they hoped to be able to put it together before the Canada Council deadline for the application. (The Council paid half the basic fee, the university the other half, but some universities paid a bit more than the basic, bringing the writer up to a salary level equal with the most junior of the professors.)

This was the way matters stood in early December, 1979. And then, apparently out of the blue, I had a phone call from Judith Miller at the University of Waterloo. She was chair of a writer-in-residence committee, she told me, and asked would I accept an appointment for 1980-81. I explained that I was already dealing with Trent, and that it was a question of their finding the money.

"We have the money right here, right now, on campus," Miller told me. "It's just a question whether you'll accept."

"Then you can call it a deal. I'll be more than willing."

I learned later that Judith had decided the university, with its associated church colleges, needed a resident writer, and had gone about getting pledges from various departments for portions of the salary. When she had some ten thousand dollars pledged, she phoned the office of the Writers' Union and asked June Callwood who was available. June said at once that I'd be the person for the job. Judith then phoned the English Department at the University of Western Ontario, and was assured that they recommended me without reservation.

The University of Waterloo, which had not had a resident writer in the past fifteen years, then applied to the Canada Council. Trent applied at the same time. The two applications arrived on the desk of the officer for writing and publication on the same day. But I had already committed myself to Waterloo, and had made no commitment to Trent, so there was no question of a choice. As it turned out, my appointment was a crucial event, both for me and the university. For me it was the beginning of an association with a group of students and writers that continued for more than three years, the foundation of a new literary journal which proved to be a permanent contribution to Canadian culture, and the opportunity to help a number of writers at the beginnings of their careers. It even led me to a collaboration with one graduate student on two books that helped to finance my more serious writing.

Once again, I worked hard at being writer-in-residence. I was determined, if possible, to make the position important enough to the university to insure that it would continue for other writers in the future. Apparently I succeeded because I was invited to stay for a second year and was consulted on the question of other appointments that were made later. I have always felt that residencies are more important than the arts awards of the Canada Council. They get some university money into arts funding, give the writer the equivalent of an arts award at half the cost to the Council, and make it possible for senior writers and beginning writers to share their knowledge.

That same year I was enrolled in the Order of Canada. The neighbours at Upper Clements were most impressed when I began getting phone calls from Rideau Hall before we even had our telephone installed. The honour was a complete surprise to me. I have never known who put forward my name—just that it wasn't the Mowats. The installation was my first meeting with Governor General Ed Schreyer and his wife Lily, but far from the last. Over the next three or four years, along with Farley and Claire, I was a frequent guest of the Schreyers and travelled with them when they visited Newfoundland and Prince Edward Island. Ed even invited me to fly with him on a Canadian Forces plane to the North Pole, but I ducked that one. I've never felt that the North Pole is worth all that bother.

Ed must have been the most unconventional Governor General in the history of the office. While I was at Government House he did such things as escape through a hole in the fence and go cross-country skiing with me without the knowledge of the security guards. He would mix drinks for his guests and serve them himself, just as if he'd been at home in Manitoba. He tried, without success, to teach Farley and me to play pool. Their son Toban enjoyed serving at table, in place of one of the staff. Lily was known to go into the kitchen and help with the cooking. She even did this once in Great Britain, when she took the Queen into the kitchens to show her how to make a traditional Ukranian dish. It was believed to be the first time the kitchens at Buckingham Palace had been graced by the royal presence since the time of Queen Anne.

My early months at Waterloo were extremely trying. I had to work very hard at the residency, and I needed one full day every week in Toronto putting the Union back together. Andrew started kindergarten in a school that proved to be completely unsuitable, with a teacher whose ideas belonged in the nineteenth century. Sexism was taught as part of the curriculum. Everyone was turned loose in the playground without supervision, while the teachers enjoyed their break indoors. Children were literally locked out of the school until the staff was ready to have them march in line to their classrooms. Christians, Jews, and Pagans alike were expected to stand and recite the Lord's Prayer and sing O Canada. And so on and so on.

We were living on campus in a visiting professor's apartment in the "married students' quarters," blocks of depressingly bleak flats with white painted walls, security locks on outside doors, and new mail-order furniture. Corky not only hated it, but kept saying so, a hundred times a day. Unlike me, she didn't have the tutoring and the writing workshops to relieve the monotony, or the weekly scramble to get the union work completed in Toronto. At the Christmas break she decided to go back to Nova Scotia, where Ellie and Jesse were keeping house for us. Once at home she decided to stay there, while Ellie went back to Newfoundland.

Though I suffered from loneliness in the empty apartment, and tried to relieve its bleakness with a few house plants and posters, the rest of the year was increasingly easy for me. I made a trip home at the mid-year break.

Andrew didn't return to school until the following September, when he enrolled in the really progressive school at Annapolis Royal, with its gifted principal, Stuart Hannam. The existence of this school in the place we had chosen to live was absolutely providential. After a year in primary Andrew spent four years in a special class with never more than nine students and a really exceptional teacher, Maureen Delaney, who was a specialist in teaching kids with "learning disabilities." Perhaps just as important as her special training, she loved kids of the age she was teaching—around eight to eleven—and gave them a sense of self-worth. I visited her classes often. (Her door was always open—you could just walk in.) Sometimes I helped her a little, once or twice showed a slide show, made friends with her kids, many of whom were exceptionally bright and intelligent, and some of whom visited us at home. Her teaching benefitted dyslexics enormously. A number of them were later able to tackle advanced levels of education that otherwise they never would have approached. Unfortunately government cuts to education later forced Delaney into a regular classroom, where she could still do much good, but not nearly as much as she was capable of.

As the year at Waterloo progressed, I was running a large writing workshop at a lounge attached to the Integrated Studies Programme. Integrated Studies was a new kind of university experience for me—a student-run department where people chose their own course of studies from the various disciplines offered on campus, or even from neighbouring universities, and pursued their studies in their own way with the help of degree supervisors and resource persons. Needless to say, the students at Integrated Studies were decidedly superior people, self-directed, self-confident, and working at things they wanted to do, rather than at spoon-fed school work. I soon found myself developing friendships among those concerned with such things as the environment, social issues, the peace movement, alternative medicine—as a group they belonged to the "Aquarian conspiracy" as it was called—in other words, they were people who had learned something from the great legacy of the sixties, and were not trying to crawl back into the Diefenbaker era, as so many mainline students were then doing. After months of preparatory work, with the help of a large committee from our own university, Wilfred Laurier University (also in Waterloo), the church colleges and the community, we brought out the first issue of *The New Quarterly* in the spring of 1981. Though published on campus, and with help from various departments, it was not a university magazine. It stood on its own, a new Canadian literary quarterly, published because we believed there were too few markets for new Canadian writing. We started with small financing. A group in Toronto, trying to launch a successor to *Tamarack Review* had announced that they needed over a hundred thousand dollars before they could begin. We laughed at this. We would begin, and pay our writers, with whatever resources came to hand. I managed to squeeze a thousand dollars out of my budget. Edna Staebler put up another thousand. Farley Mowat donated a thousand. The university departments managed to scrounge about a thousand between them, amounts varying from $150 to $300 each.

I insisted that our writers had to be paid decently by the standards of "little" magazines. I was not prepared to see *The New Quarterly* join the parade of literary journals who paid their authors little or nothing, and spent their money, instead, on fancy covers, glossy paper, and professional typesetting. All our work—printing, cutting, binding, as well as editing and proof-reading—was done by volunteers. Because no one department was ever asked for more than a few hundred dollars at a time, and the requests came no oftener than once a year, we were able to remain afloat without having to go back to private contributors. From the beginning, we paid $100 for a short story, or more, and this put us among the best literary markets in Canada! One well-known writer told me that her first cheque from *The New Quarterly* was the largest single payment for her work she had ever received.

For the first few years we did it without government subsidies of any kind. After we had published twelve quarterly issues, the Ontario Arts Council began giving us a grant. It was seven years before the Canada Council finally deigned to recognize our existence. Meanwhile, we had published work by a veritable who's who of established Canadian writers, and had introduced the work of about forty new writers who were being published at the very beginning of their careers. In 1990 the magazine began its tenth year of publication with a 326-page special issue on Mennonite writing. By then it was established as one of the major literary quarterlies in Canada, with its contributors winning national awards every year.

When the writer-in-residence committee invited me back for a second year, I didn't return to the professor's flat in the married student quarters. Instead, I went to live with a group of students who were sharing a rented house. At first there was no bedroom available, and most of the basement space had already been preempted by two temporary rooms, both occupied, so I built a rough bunk in a broom closet, and ran a wire into it for illumination. We had a large sitting room and a kitchen and three upstairs bedrooms. Two mated students might share a bed, and there was often someone sleeping in the sitting room, so we usually had eight people, sometimes more. It was not at all unpleasant. We shared all the cooking and housework evenly, ate only vegetarian food, and got away with a very small rent payment. (I think I paid $50 a month.) The people who lived there were all gifted and intelligent. It was, of course, a far more satisfactory place to be than any married students quarters. Eventually, when someone moved away, I was next in line for a bedroom, and slept in luxury for the rest of the year. But the broom closet wasn't abandoned. Another student promptly moved in. Thanks to Edna Staebler, my diet wasn't exclusively vegetarian, and I often shared lunch with Judith Miller at a campus cafeteria.

While I was in residence, Judith and I brought a parade of high-profile authors to the campus for readings, workshops, and, in the case of Alice Munro, for weekend-long meetings with students and faculty. Even Alden Nowlan, who had then reached the point where he just wasn't going anywhere very often, came at my invitation, and made a tremendous hit with the students.

As the end of my second year approached, a staff vacancy appeared at Integrated Studies. Dr. Anne Innis Dagg, one of the resource people, was leaving for a year in Australia. A group of students persuaded me to apply, and I was elected in competition with a long list of highly qualified academics. So I had a third year at Waterloo, during which I continued my writing workshops, and held a series of seminars on science, history, and other subjects. Graeme Gibson, at my suggestion, took the residency at Waterloo that year, and was very popular with the fledgling writers (students and faculty) whose ambitions I had been abetting.

I again lived with a group of students, this time in the Daggs' house, which was vacant for a year while Anne and her husband pursued research projects in Australia. It was right on the edge of Waterloo Park, a couple of blocks from the main business square—ideally located. Again, the students were simply wonderful. One of them later assured me that she had learned more from "the seminars at the breakfast table" than she had from the university lectures. Leaving it all behind was one of the saddest events of my life.

But I regretfully decided in the spring of 1983 not to return in September. Though I could get home for a week fairly often, I was spending too much time away from my family and from the patch of ground that I cared so much about on the shore of Annapolis Basin. So I returned to Nova Scotia full-time. Even more than I expected, I missed the students. For the first time in my life I began to feel old. It has to happen sooner or later, and I suppose you are lucky if it doesn't begin before you are in your sixties.

I left the Writers' Union in great shape. The campaign to secure public lending right was on track. The Canada Council was now on side in this respect, and I knew it was just a matter of time before the government agreed. A committee headed by Andreas Schroeder eventually worked out the details, but it was the groundwork laid by Marian Engel among librarians, teachers, publishers and cultural agencies that made it possible. Before leaving office, I was able to assure union members through the newsletter that public lending right was on the way.

Since payments were based on library holdings, they rewarded productive writers whose books were carried by libraries, not just a few high-profile ones known to the media. For the first time in Canada even poets could count on a few dollars of basic income so long as libraries bought their books.

The union also did great service in opposing censorship, promoting the freedom to read, limiting the American practice of dumping publishers' overruns on the Canadian market while Canadian editions were still selling, and in securing a fair share of the market for women writers and writers from ethnic minorities.

It took many years to establish protection of copyright against unlimited photocopying, but that too was achieved in time. Finally, the concept of culture as an important, labour-intensive industry, an industry basic to the economic as well as the spiritual health of the nation, penetrated even the halls of power. This concept had been formed and propagated by members of the Writers' Union of Canada, without whom culture would still have been regarded as something allied to the morning coffee break and the afternoon bridge club.

One of my students at Waterloo was a woman named Dona Massel, a dyslexic who nevertheless accumulated enough credits, bit by bit, to graduate with an English degree. She eventually published several slim volumes of verses, and a remarkable religious play, something between a mystery play and a pageant, that I saw performed by a huge costumed cast in a church. This woman not only managed to cope with dyslexia, but also recovered from an accident that almost killed her, eventually survived brain surgery and returned after about a year to a normal life. In addition to her writing and publishing, she organized a writing workshop and a reading circle, not at the university but in the city of Kitchener. Such a legacy from a writer's residency at a university is, of course, very rare, but it is the kind of thing that makes the effort worthwhile. By her various activities, which all originated in a writing workshop that I conducted on campus, Dona Massel has permanently enriched the cultural life of her city and her region.

The New Quarterly, of course, was my most visible legacy. It has published numerous young writers, many of them for the first time, and some of them have gone on to achieve great success. As I write this, the editors have just brought out a 208-page special issue devoted to the work of John Metcalf and his students. It does not make as much noise as its predecessor, the *Tamarack Review*, but over the past eighteen years it has done great work in the co-operative effort of building the Canadian bibliography.

My connection with the university didn't end with my return to Nova Scotia. Not only did the writer-in-residence committee continue to seek my advice, but students, singly and in groups, came visiting. Those were all post-grads, intellectual, often brilliant, thoroughly "hip to the jive" as we used to say back in the '60s. They came to talk, to discuss plans, to visit with a family that was living its dream, not caught up in the rat race. Some of them managed to escape the rat race themselves, took up occupations like alternative medicine or freelance editing. One young man built his own sailing yacht, junk-rigged, on the coast of northern Vancouver Island. At least two resorted to Mennonite-style farming in their home province. And such alternative lifestyles were not necessarily transient. Some of those who graduated twenty years ago are still living independent lives on the fringes of the dreadful society that we have imposed upon ourselves in North America. They aren't wealthy, but by God they're far happier than the ones who were herded off to work for the transnational corporations.

I was asked by my old department, Integrated Studies, to be academic advisor for some of their students. I judged literary contests (though I don't, on principle, believe in them). The connection went on and on. Eventually I had to drop such activities—most recently I rejected an offer to tour Latin America. When you get into your mid-seventies, you had best learn to slow down.

Chapter 14

During the 1980s at Annapolis Basin I wrote two books in addition to the popular histories Ed Butts and I produced together, and the regional histories that I wrote for Breakwater Books and Oxford University Press. These were *Dancing on the Shore* and *Joey*.

People who admired *The Foxes of Beachy Cove* often wondered why I had never written a sequel. There were several reasons. Perhaps the strongest was that I find it hard to write a sequel to anything. None of my books has ever had a sequel. There was no second novel about life in the Newfoundland outports, none about northern Labrador or the Arctic, and no second "nature book." I had said what I had to say about the square mile of Beachy Cove and its creatures once and for all. But Annapolis Basin was a wholly new kind of place, my reading over the intervening twenty years had produced many new ideas, or expanded old ones, and I had reached the point where I wasn't afraid to diverge a bit from the well-trodden pathways of ortho-dox science.

While I was going about my business of developing a garden and a park on the shore of Annapolis Basin, a sudden insight into the nature of things would arise out of my work, and I'd rush back to my office to jot it down on the typewriter in a paragraph or two. Then I'd go about my work once more. At the same time, I was filling the margins of my books, especially those dealing with the evolution of life and the nature of the universe, with marginalia and footnotes—notes that often amplified what the writer said, or diverged from it, or contradicted it entirely. At some point I began adding the marginalia and footnotes to the notes in my file, and those notes gradually grew from a few paragraphs to a few pages devoted to each subject. At first I wasn't at all sure that I had the makings of a book. But when I began reworking the material I found that it fell easily into chapters. Moreover, I discovered that I had invented a structure: my essays would begin with some local incident or observation, such as paddling a canoe on the Basin, working among bees and clover, examining a pond through the glass-clear ice of winter. But following that, they would move from the local to the general, and on from the general to the theoretical, so that I might begin by describing the colours of a finch, and within a page or two I would find myself discussing the motive power behind the evolution of life, or the human place in the flow of energy from hydrogen atom to living galaxy. A number of readers later remarked that this was a structure they had never seen before. But I didn't invent it. It just happened.

It was very satisfying work, and easy to do so long as you weren't in a hurry, but I was far from sure that it would ever make a book until I had some twenty pieces completed. Then I began sorting them, to see if there was a common theme, and some way of fitting them together. A few of them I had to set aside, perhaps for future use, somewhere else. Others I had to expand and integrate, but eventually the theme emerged, and the overall integration took place.

I had never done anything like this before. I didn't write the book. It accumulated. But when I had finished a draft it pleased me more than anything I had done with the possible exception of *Remembering Summer*. My old friend Doug Gibson, who had recently moved from Macmillan to McClelland and Stewart, was enormously impressed, and immediately offered to publish it.

Doug, who had gradually built up a great reputation as an editor, was now publishing under his own imprint in a publishing house that was also under new management. He edited the book himself, and I must give him credit—he used the greatest care and enthusiasm, and saw it meticulously through the press. I never had a book more carefully and lovingly produced.

At my suggestion G. Brender à Brandis, who had used some of my earlier writing to accompany his artwork, contributed his beautiful wood engravings as decorations. The finished product was everything that I could have hoped, and the people of the Annapolis Valley took the book to their hearts in a way that I never expected. More than a hundred of my neighbours in this sparsely settled region came out to buy autographed copies of *Dancing on the Shore* on the day it was "launched" at Upper Clements.

While this was going on I also worked at such breadwinners as the book on the Newfoundland Rangers and the social history of Corner Brook. A curious result of the latter was that we began making annual motor trips to the southern Atlantic states. Bowater's, who were financing the research on the Corner Brook history, asked me to go to a number of places in Connecticut, Tennessee and South Carolina to interview senior employees of theirs who had formerly worked at their Corner Brook mill. It so happened that I went by car at the end of March, taking Corky, Andrew and Leah with me. After visiting Bowater people in Connecticut, we travelled southwards through the mountains of Tennessee, camping there in wonderful spring weather, and then on the offshore islands of Pamlico Sound, North Carolina. The redbuds and the flowering dogwoods were just coming to the peak of their bloom; the gardens of South Carolina, where we visited Bowater's North American headquarters, were ablaze with azaleas; the beaches were so pleasant that we went swimming in the sea, and acquired a touch of sunburn. All this within two days drive of home! Then and there we decided to go again in following years.

We varied our trips. We drove south through the mountains one year, north one year along the Blue Ridge Parkway. One year we crossed Delaware Bay by ferry. At other times we went by way of the Chesapeake Bay bridge and tunnel. Just once we drove north through every major city from Richmond and Washington to Boston, all in one day—an experience I would never want to repeat.

We found camping places almost unknown to the flocks of "snowbirds": Goose Creek, for instance, in North Carolina, and a beautiful beach with an unserviced campground in the Croatan National Forest. The kids collected fossils at Edisto Beach and photographed alligators in the Huntington Beach lagoon. Leah compiled a bird list that would have done credit to an adult naturalist.

We camped not only in sub-tropical weather, but also in spectacular thunderstorms, and once we took refuge from tornados under a highway overpass. We had one wet trip out of ten, but even then the weather was pleasant most of the time.

The year following the Bowater research we headed for Hunting Island as fast as we could get there. We had never heard of the place, just picked it off the map, but discovered immediately that this offshore camping park at the southern tip of South Carolina is one of the most attractive places on the Atlantic Coast: miles of sunny sand, thousands of migrating birds, pelicans diving for fish, oysters that you can collect and cook for your supper, dolphins cruising past, limitless amounts of dead wood that you can collect for campfires, seawater that is sometimes warm even in March, miles of sand dunes, a forest of mixed palms and pines, a large tidal marsh, animals that you could never see further north. Once we had been there we included a stop at Hunting Island in every one of our subsequent trips.

Our first experience of Florida was not encouraging. We drove south along the coastal highway past a thousand fast-food joints, ten thousand billboards, and wall-to-wall motels facing a seawall with steps dropping down to the beaches that had nothing to offer beyond the occasional stranded jellyfish. We were heading south to visit our neighbors Bill and Vina Percy, who had a winter cottage near Melbourne. If this was Florida, we decided, we didn't really want to see any more of it. But then we discovered the wonderful surf beach and lagoon at Sebastian Inlet—the lagoon a fascinating nursery of wildlife ranging from nudibranchs to huge horseshoe crabs. And then we discovered the dry uplands.

In fact, Florida in early spring can be wonderful if you stay away from such obvious places as Miami and Tampa and Daytona Beach, and, of course, Orlando and Disney World. On our third or fourth trip south we discovered Florida's Ocala National Forest.

The fountains that arise in the flat lands of the Florida pine forests are no ordinary backyard springs. Entire rivers come surging up through layers of limestone, creating crystal pools of swirling water, so you can swim above a vertical cavern and look down to the depths to see purple fish, full fathom five, cruising across a bottom of white sand. Turtles and garfish drift past, from pod to pod of water weeds, and little blue herons perch in the trees gulping small prey caught in the shallows. The water wells out of the earth sometimes in small sand boils that spit out fossilized sharks' teeth, sometimes in floods that will float a ship. This land that is often bone-dry for months at a stretch absorbs enough rain to replenish its deep reservoirs and to keep the limpid springs forever flowing for turtle and water snake and snowy egret resplendent in lacy plumes, and even for the rare manatee that makes its way upriver to wallow like some prehistoric monster in the equable warmth of summer water in midwinter. Once having visited this region—Silver Glen Springs, Juniper Springs, Manatee Springs on the Suwanee River to the northwest—we decided to include it in every subsequent journey to the south. We were lucky with the wildlife, too. Though we failed to see such obvious things as wild turkeys (which we stalked in vain) we were visited by a dancing armadillo, watched tiny southern deer the size of collie dogs grazing in forest clearings, found the nest of a pair of barred owls, and even watched courting limpkins in a cypress swamp—birds that were all but exterminated by the spraying of herbicides to control the growth of water hyacinths. The limpkins depend for food on the apple snails, which depend in turn on the water weeds that get in the way of powerboats—so the water weeds have to go, and the snails and limpkins along with them. In the American scheme of things powerboats have priority. Apple snails and limpkins are expendable.

We did not confine our camping to southern states in the months of March and April. Our kids grew up in tents almost as much as in the house. We camped all over Nova Scotia from early May to September, explored beaches and caves and the hills that are locally called mountains. We camped in summer in Ontario and upstate New York. We camped annually in Newfoundland. In the summer of 1983 1 took Andrew and Robin (the boy from the Beachy Cove cabin) to Northern Bay Sands, and then on to Baccalieu Island, where we saw thousands of colonial nesting birds and pods of great whales. That same year we did the hike through the Nova Scotia forest to Cape Split and back twice. Andrew and I even did the hike barefooted. He went with me to Lord's Cove on the Burin Peninsula, where we helped to take a basking shark out of a cod trap—his first experience in a trap boat on the open sea, and it was a dandy! The skipper was surprised that he didn't get seasick. We came back at night in a "good lop" when we saw the water "burn" and splashes of phosphorescence coming over the gunwales. That summer Andrew collected some beautiful rocks—among others, a fine chunk of amethyst and a large geode with quartz crystals.

That year, too, Corky and I dug our second, larger pond, by hand with spades, leaving islands, but producing a lovely sheet of water in the lower part of our ravine, and that winter the kids began using it for skating. The pond involved a tremendous amount of work, especially when I had to haul out, by hand, clumps of large willows, but when it was completed it added immensely to the beauty of the grounds, and not only gave the kids and their friends a place to skate in winter, but a place to use inflatable boats in summer. It attracted frogs, herons, and even a pair of muskrats, which we had to drive away because they dug holes through our dam.

Next year I finished the downstairs greenhouse, a sort of small conservatory, with brick planters, a stone floor, and a fish pond among the rocks at one end.

On September 10, 1986 we drove to Vermont on the first leg of a camping trip that was to take us to Vancouver Island once again, to visit Rozie, who had lived with us at Annapolis Royal for three years, and was now living at Tofino where she had a boat, a man and a job in the hospital.

We drove to Niagara Falls through New York State, then north to Waterloo for a reunion with Edna Staebler on September 13. Next day we crossed the border at Port Huron and camped among huge sand dunes on the lakeshore just north of Chicago. Then we visited Corky's sister, Mary Ann and her husband Harold Gilomen at their farm in southern Minnesota.

In South Dakota we camped at a place called Thunder Basin, which lived up to its name by producing a ring of thunderstorms at night, all around the horizon, though not a drop of rain fell where we were camped. We also visited Crystal

Cave, and a park in the badlands among fantastic rock formations where Andrew began making the first of his many hundreds of nature photographs. On September 19 we hiked across the lava field known as the Craters of the Moon in central Idaho, and the next day crossed by ferry to Nanaimo on Vancouver Island. At Tofino the kids got to explore a bit of temperate rain forest, and to see the fantastic rock pools of the Pacific beaches.

Once more we drove southward along the coasts of Washington and Oregon to California and camped among the great redwoods. On September 29 we got lost trying to cross the high Sierras among the snows of an extra early winter, and much to our surprise wound up on the same side of the range from which we had started, but later that same day we were in the central valley of California camping beside a giant fig tree and eating all the ripe figs and wild grapes and walnuts we could hold. Next day we saw the incredible stone formations in Red Rock Canyon, and on October 1 drove through Death Valley to Lake Mead.

As we continued eastward there were deer and pronghorn antelopes and big horned sheep—then the fantastic rocks of the Grand Canyon and the Petrified Forest and the Painted Desert—once again, a visual experience never to be forgotten. On October 4 we got across the Arkansas River just ahead of a flood that was closing highways all over the region.

Here we took a short detour through the Ozark hills, discovering to our delight that things had changed little since pioneer days. There were tiny cabins with goats in the yards, long, lean mountaineers lounging in the sun, two barefoot boys cleaving wood with double-bitted axes, women and girls hardly visible at all—just glimpsed from time to time in open doorways. At one place there was even an outdoor stone oven for baking bread.

On October 7 we decided to stay over for a full day at Tim's Ford in Tennessee; here we all went swimming, and Andrew for the first time really managed to swim with a fairly convincing dog's paddle. He has always insisted that his lean, bony build makes swimming difficult. On October 8 he went swimming again at South Holston Lake on the Virginia-Tennessee border, and from that day forward he and Leah were both swimming successfully.

This trip we visited Harper's Ferry, and saw both the nineteenth century village and a great collection of ruins. We then camped at Falling Waters in West Virginia, where the kids collected a huge bag of black walnuts. On October 10 we put up at a motel in Mystic, Connecticut—only the fourth night we had spent in motels that trip—and the next day drove to Saint John. Altogether, in a journey of thirty-two days, we had spent twenty-one nights in camp, much of it in bad weather. It rained in the Badlands. It rained in Idaho. It rained at the Grand Canyon, it rained in the Painted Desert, it rained in the Petrified Forest and in western Texas. On no other camping trip did we have such consistently bad luck with the weather, but we had a glorious time. Corky always goes camping well prepared with tarpaulins and extra ropes for bad weather shelters, so we can enjoy picnics and camp fires even in the rain.

That year I published four books in three months: *Corner Brook* and *The Rangers* with Breakwater, *Remembering Summer* with Pottersfield, and *Historic Newfoundland* with Oxford. McClelland and Stewart had accepted *Dancing on the Shore* for publication the following autumn, and Doubleday were planning to publish *Bandits and Privateers* as a sequel to *Pirates and Outlaws*. Actually, both those books came out in 1987, so that I had no less than six books published in a year and a half. This, of course, is not good policy. When you publish books in clusters you are competing with yourself.

Historic Newfoundland began with John de Visser's photography. He had been fascinated since his first visit with the photogenic qualities of the island, and had collected an impressive array of beautiful slides. He sent me prints, and suggested that we had the makings of a book. After arranging them in a kind of historical order, I could see certain blank spots, which I pointed out to John. He then went for one more trip to Newfoundland, and sent me the results. I was now able to arrange his pictures in an unbroken historical sequence, illustrating with contemporary photographs the history cf Newfoundland from the Norse voyages to the present. A generous caption with each photograph provided a connected chronological text covering a period of almost a thousand years. I was delighted with the book. It was visually pleasing, and condensed the history of Newfoundland into a compass that you could read, with its accompanying pictures, in a couple of hours. The format made it easy for readers of any age.

The Rangers, Corner Brook, Historic Newfoundland, Pirates and Outlaws, and Bandits and Privateers were all extremely easy books to write, and all profitable. In the first year of publication they earned me, between them, some $50,000, the fruits of working time that could not have exceeded ten or eleven months. Consequently, during the eighties I had ample leisure for other pursuits—for working on more difficult books, like Dancing on the Shore and Joey, for building my conservatories and my ornamental ponds, for laying the stone floors in the house, for travelling, and for helping Andrew to cope with dyslexia.

Dyslexia, of course, is a lifelong problem. It's not something that you "fix" with a few years of remedial reading. In Andrew's case he was very fortunate to be in a school at Annapolis Royal which had a special class for dyslexics, taught by a teacher who understood the problem thoroughly. At the same time he got a fair general education with film, discussion, videotape and so on. But he made his first real breakthrough in reading not at school, but during a camping trip in the American south. Every day during our vacation I gave him a reading lesson, using one of the remedial reading textbooks from the Department of Education. At the beginning of the trip he could scarcely manage ten words a minute. At the end of the trip he was reading twenty words a minute, and sometimes thirty.

"I never thought I'd be able to read like this," he told me. it was the beginning of constant progress. That year he was doing the equivalent of grade six in a regular classroom with some thirty boys and girls, and taking art lessons from Nina Cropas at Clementsport. I kept him out of school one morning each week for art lessons and for tutoring at home. His teacher told me that this was working out really well, but the school did not believe he was ready for junior high school in regular classrooms.

I took him for a visit to Bridgeway Academy in Wolfville, where he met the students and the principal, Karen Duncan. Bridgeway was one of two schools in Wolfville serving dyslexics. The other was Landmark East, an expensive residential school. Andrew had to decide between going to Bridgeway the following year, or going back to the junior school in Annapolis. He thought it over for a few days, and decided on Bridgeway.

I rented a small apartment in Wolfville for the next three years, moved my typewriter there, and wrote my biography of J.R. Smallwood, doing my research mostly in the library of Acadia University while Andrew worked at his reading. The first year we spent four days a week at Wolfville and three at home, Andrew studying art with Gene Samson in Annapolis Royal. His education that year cost approximately $10,000 (including rent and transportation) and we paid the whole shot out of our savings. The second year we applied for, and received, a grant from the Atlantic Provinces Special Education Authority—$4,000 for school fees. This reduced our private expenditure to about $6,000, perhaps somewhat less, because it was tax deductible. That year we spent five days a week at Wolfville, and Andrew took art lessons from Leonard Paul, a very meticulous young artist of Mi'qmaq background living in Wolfville. Leonard Paul was not at all anxious to teach, and just occasionally did a lecture for a school class. He made an exception in Andrew's case because Andrew had a learning disability and might be expected to benefit from private art lessons. This was the third of Andrew's art teachers. He learned something new and different from each of them.

His reading was improving steadily, and he had learned to write in longhand—not rapidly, but quite legibly. In addition to the books that were assigned in school, he read several at home in Wolfville. The one thing they seemed unable to teach him at Bridgeway was elementary math.

That year I completed and published *Joey*. It was a lot of hard work, but at least the source material was within easy reach. Acadia made all their facilities available to me. The only cost was my occasional use of their fax machine—a method of communication that I could willingly have done without, but that seemed essential to the editors and sales staff at General Publishers, who had bought publication rights from my agent, Bella Pomer, in Toronto. Acadia had all major Canadian newspapers on microfilm, and the newspapers had followed Joey step by step. I scanned the two St. John's papers, the *Halifax Chronicle-Herald*, and occasionally the *Globe and Mail*. There had been few days when Joey wasn't in the papers. The only danger was going blind from the flickering images on the screen. I could usually reconstruct the events behind the newspaper stories because throughout most of his twenty-five-year public career I was either directly associated with him, or else sitting in the press gallery as a reporter. Throughout that time I had been digging daily into the background, making use of my contacts in Joey's government and the police department to discover what was happening behind the scenes.

Richard Gwyn had published an account of Smallwood's political career. I didn't want merely to improve on Gwyn's work. I wanted to examine Joey's character and motivations—indeed, that was my principal aim—not just to examine, once again, the rise and fall of a Canadian Huey Long, but to discover, for myself and my readers, "what made Joey run."

On alternate days or part days I'd take my research materials and rough drafts back to the apartment on the Ridge Road above Wolfville and type it up. A second typescript gave me all the revision I needed.

The book was something of a triumph from every point of view. For the first time in my life, I had received a really generous advance against royalties. Until then, my advances had never exceeded $8,500. For *Joey* General Publishers paid $38,500, plus expenses. Dutton paid another $5,000 for American publication of *Dancing on the Shore*, so all told my earnings that year were quite respectable. Andrew and I went to Newfoundland the week of publication, and I spent many hours on radio and television in Corner Brook and St. John's.

I made a cash donation of $1000 to the Smallwood Heritage Foundation, which was publishing Joey's *Encyclopaedia of Newfoundland and Labrador*, and gave them a hundred books in advance of publication, all numbered and signed, which they sold for $50 each, for a total return to the Foundation of $6,000. I went to Roache's Line to see Joey for one last time, and he was greatly pleased with the visit. Then I spent a few days in Toronto, Ottawa, London and Kitchener-Waterloo doing promotion before returning to Wolfville. But the book was not well promoted, because General Publishers was going through major restructuring at the time. Consequently, sales never reached the levels that General Publishers had expected, but the book made a great impression in the Atlantic Provinces, where many people said it was the best thing I had written, which, of course, it was not—by a long way.

We applied for a grant for Andrew to spend a third year at Bridgeway, and again we received it. That year he did grade nine, and averaged seventy-one percent in his exams. I believed a fourth year, or more, would be beneficial—indeed, that it wouldn't hurt him a bit to go as far as grade twelve in the private school, but I was coming to the end of my own willingness to spend so much time away from home. As for Corky, she absolutely hated to have Andrew and me away for five days a week. So after much thought and discussion, we decided to have him do grade ten at home in 1990-91. Karen Duncan supported this plan, and helped us by supplying special reading materials.

Actually, that was the year Andrew really took off. His reading was still slow, but he had great patience and application, and tackled a string of books, some of them well beyond high-school level, went through them all successfully, and wrote excellent book reports on each as he finished it. My own feeling was that except for math he was doing far better than grade ten work—things more at university level. He produced, among other things, a term paper on the structure of the solar system that would have done credit to any university freshman. Karen Duncan was amazed by it. "Did you really write this, Andrew?" she asked.

I gave him assignments in practical math, and he managed to complete them with the help of a calculator—a skill that he later used when he passed his examination for a radio operator's license. I also taught him deductive geometry—a branch of mathematics no longer taught in Canadian schools, but in my opinion most important because it is a direct approach to logic, and hence to all the higher levels of science. The simplistic linear thinking that plagues so much of our science is probably a result of people having approached mathematics only by way of algebra. Andrew's work that year included thirteen theorems based on Euclid, and for this he showed a decided aptitude, producing meticulous diagrams with faultless deductions. I also showed him some practical applications. He was able, for instance, to measure the vertical height of any object by the use of triangulation—a power pole, a building, a hill. His year at home was the most successful school year he had ever completed. Among other studies we included basic books on science and engineering. Each of those books had lengthy "before and after" tests to show how much you had learned. He scored close to 100% in both. Severe dyslexia, at Andrew's level, is for the vast majority of people a lifelong sentence of illiteracy. And it isn't something you "fix" with a set of headphones or sheets of coloured plastic or any of the other tricks that have been promoted as "the answer." It is a struggle with circuitry in the brain that can only be confronted by many years of hard work, by finding paths around the problem instead of trying to "fix" it. In his case, by the great good fortune of living in a place where special education was available, and by having parents who knew how to help, he learned to cope with the handicap, and to become a functional reader able to handle two or three books a month by the age of sixteen, and to acquire an excellent general education at the same time. Adults who met him were invariably astonished by the depth and breadth of his knowledge.

There were some advantages to spending five days a week in Wolfville. For one thing, being a university town it had more to offer in the arts than a rural village such as Annapolis Royal. Andrew and I were able to attend classical concerts by soloists, chamber groups, and even a symphony orchestra. The university art gallery mounted a new exhibition every six weeks or so. Every year there would be at least two or three stage productions worth seeing.

The countryside also had something to offer. You have to go a long way from the Annapolis Basin to find any decent inland canoe water. At Wolfville it is next door in the Gaspereau Valley. It was also much better than Annapolis for bicycles. In spring and autumn we rode across the dykes on numerous occasions as far as Grand Pré or Evangeline Beach–ten or twelve miles in an afternoon. I also began riding while Andrew was in school—up and down hill from the Ridge Road to the dyke lands on the one side or the Gaspereau Valley on the other. Compared to the continuous thundering of heavy trucks on the road between Annapolis Royal and Digby, the motor traffic on those roads was relatively light. I soon got to the point where I was riding fifteen or twenty miles, or even more, every day.

Andrew had insisted, as soon as we went to Wolfville, that he wanted a mountain bike. He made the first major expenditure from his bank account to buy one—a reasonably good model for which he paid $440 in Halifax. It was so superior to my old three-speed, or to the ten-speed racing bike that I'd picked up at Wolfville, that I bought two of them—cheaper models than Andrew's, but still adequate. In theory, Corky and I would share one bike, and Leah ride the other. In fact Leah did a lot of riding—often between Upper Clements and Annapolis Royal. But Corky used the bike very little, while I used it a lot. The return to Upper Clements cut sharply into my cycling. It's just not a very good place for a bicycle. Indeed, Andrew and I had the experience of being knocked into a ditch, both of us, by a passing car, while we rode on the shoulder, well off the pavement. Neither of us was hurt in the sideswipe; even the bicycles received little damage, but the car smashed itself full-speed into a nearby concrete culvert. The driver said he had passed out at the wheel. Six inches further off the road, and he would have killed both of us. It was a long time before Andrew would ride again on a road frequented by motor traffic, but he did, eventually, riding all over Vancouver and its environs for some weeks in 1998.

The return to Upper Clements gave me much more time to work in the garden, at firewood, and at the house. I did extensive stonework and brickwork in both greenhouses. I bought a large used Roto-tiller, and gave up ploughing with the tractor. We brought several new patches of ground into production, improved the ponds, and planted dozens of flowering shrubs, Andrew built a large raft for use on the Basin, and a lookout platform in the trees beside the beach. We drained and dug our largest pond to install six-mil building plastic to make the water level more controllable. Eventually, we had a large school of goldfish in this pond, and flowering plants in and around it.

The rather frantic life of commuting to Wolfville, working against publishers' deadlines to finish *Joey*, and then getting it into print, caused stress symptoms that bothered me for some months. A specialist reassured me that nothing was seriously wrong, and the symptoms disappeared when I began taking it easier at home. I got back to writing these memoirs, and at the same time writing a sequel to *Dancing on the Shore*—both at a leisurely pace.

We had, by now, no financial worries. At the end of 1990 we had bought a new mini-van ($22,000) for cash, and had $115,000 in savings with no indebtedness. Care, prudence and luck during the great bull market of the 1980s and 90s had created our financial security with the help of a friendly broker in Halifax—Paul Conrad. Our children's demands were very modest. Apart from Andrew's education, they wanted almost nothing: such odds and ends as a colour TV, a VCR, a small microscope, a pair of field glasses. We never denied them anything they asked for, but they had sense enough not to ask for the garbage that most North American kids covet, as they are trained to do on TV. Between the two of them, they had savings of more than $10,000 (partly from their grandparents' estate) which they never touched, and which continued to increase. By 1999 Leah had paid for two years of university without having to work on the side, and Andrew had a "net worth" of well over $100,000.

We were never in a state of conflict with our children. This puzzled the school greatly. They sent home questionnaires asking what rules kids' parents enforced, how often they were "grounded" or otherwise punished, where they were allowed to go, and when. Etc. We were only able to reply that none of it applied to our family—there *were* no rules; nobody ever "earned privileges" or was "grounded" for misbehaviour, or was ever threatened or intimidated—a regime that seems to prevail in most North American families. Our children were self-directed, but depended very largely on our advice in spite of that fact—or perhaps because of it. From our point of view, when they reached the ages of fourteen and sixteen, they could hardly have been more satisfactory people to live with.

Leah "went in" for a lot of stuff at school, and tended to fret about the fact that she had to skip school for three or four weeks every spring in order to accompany us on our trips to the south—sometimes also in the autumn for a trip across the continent. She played flute in the school band, played in the chess club (fourth place) and represented the Annapolis region in long-distance running. She tried out for badminton, went hiking and canoeing with a scout troop. All this was done with no encouragement from her parents, who tended to resent having to drive her to those extracurricular activities several times a week. As soon as possible she took a driving course, and began using the mini-van.

Andrew's achievements were quieter. He became expert with axe and saw and pruning shears, created a brook with little falls along its course in our ravine, dug a spare well by hand (useful for watering one of our gardens), had two of his pictures hung at the Canadian National Exhibition, sold others for book jackets, picked up a first-class certificate in social studies, bought a good professional camera, and became an outstanding nature photographer. He also acquired really excellent taste in music. We already had some one hundred and thirty classical tapes, which he played. He added some classic rock from the sixties and a wide-ranging collection of "ethnic" music, some of it from China, Japan, the Arab world, and even central Asia. He became a fan of international radio, and bought the best multi-wave receiver he could find. Soon he was corresponding with stations in Egypt, China, Japan, and many other places. During the Gulf War we didn't depend on the American propaganda broadcasts (all you could get in Canada). We got our war news, in English, from Egypt. By his early twenties, Andrew was writing a detailed travel journal which we found fascinating, and producing piles of science fiction. Though he had been licensed to drive since the age of seventeen, he still hadn't bought a car by the age of twenty-five, and rarely sat behind a wheel except as a spare driver on long trips.

We continued camping, summer and winter. In 1991 we camped for the first time on St. George Island, on the north shore of the Gulf of Mexico, and were delighted with the many miles of white beaches, and the great flocks of birds of species we had never seen before. In August of that year while one of Corky's daughters and her husband and two kids stayed at our place in Upper Clements trying to keep ahead of the harvests from the garden, we motored across the continent once again to visit Rozie on the west coast of Vancouver Island, and to see for the first time a pair of two-year-old twin grandchildren who, unlike all our other grandchildren, proved to be holy terrors. I slept in a houseboat, went swimming on a "free" beach, and waded short distances through nearly impassable rain forest.

Andrew made beautiful photographs of the spectacular scenery, and of wildlife, and of tide pools. But nothing seemed to hold his interest for long. Once he'd done something difficult, like photographing a spider at a range of two inches, he never wanted to repeat the procedure. He had ceased drawing and painting, except to illustrate his science fiction stories. He had no impulse for "getting and spending," either. A small income from a modest-sized portfolio seemed to satisfy him. None of this bothered me all that much. I remembered myself as a teenager and in my twenties, filling notebooks with drawings (for which I had no aptitude at all) writing orchestral and vocal music (for which I had no training) writing reams of poetry, hiking twenty miles at a stretch, plunging into politics, organizing trade unions, leading public debates, and so on. Andrew might eventually decide whether he wants to do one thing more than others.

Leah, meanwhile, went off to Norway with a guy named Tor Gjesdal, and had her first baby there on Christmas Eve 1998. I could wish nothing better for any of my friends than that they could have two such children.

Andrew's science fiction stories circulated among members of our extended family, all of whom found them interesting enough, but he didn't seem to be heading toward really major writing until the early months of 1999. Then he sat down with pen and pencil for about twelve hours a day, and produced, in a period of six months, an absolutely astonishing novel of great power and sensitivity, eighty-five thousand words of faultless prose in a truly mature style, and totally original in concept. He hasn't yet gone looking for a publisher, but I'm sure he will find one.

Corky? Well, she'd like to spend all her time travelling, but we have to spend at least part of our time at home so I can continue writing, and so we can continue looking after our increasing population of plants, cats and wild birds. Late in life Corky discovered that she likes long-distance driving, and has made five or six singlehanded drives from Annapolis Basin to Beachy Cove (over a thousand miles each way). As I write this she is contemplating driving alone to British Columbia.

Chapter 15

When I reached the age of seventy in 1993 I was far from finished with writing. I come from a long-lived family, and a long line of writers. My son Andrew is the fourth generation of writers in our family, starting with his great grandfather, who wrote marine history, his grandfather, who published three books, his uncle, who published two, and his cousin John, who writes texts for college use.

I had at least four books to come, but I'd had no book published since *Joey*, in 1989, and none was ready for publication. I sent outlines of books I was trying to write to my agent, Bella Pomer, in Toronto, and Bella tried them on various publishers without any encouraging response. Perhaps, I thought, the kind of book I wanted to write was no longer in demand.

My outline for *A Natural History of the Atlantic Provinces* went to many publishers from Vancouver to St. John's without finding a sponsor. Some of them said they would love to publish it, but couldn't afford a book with numerous full-page colour photographs. The day of the great coffee-table book was over. Those still appearing were heavily subsidized by corporations, governments, or such environmental organizations as the Sierra Club.

The response to *Earth and High Heaven*, the projected final volume of my nature writing, was little better. In disgust with it all I put everything aside and began writing a series of connected short stories—about the life of a man born in Brigus in the

1920s. If I couldn't write for publication, then I might as well write for my own pleasure. I started with a couple of brief stories about a boy's first tentative sexual awakening, and his early experiences afloat and ashore. I projected fifteen stories, spent two years writing and revising them, and in the end did sixteen. I was very pleased with the result: a gentle, poetic, episodic novel that I intended to call *Snipe Flight and Evening Light*, but that was eventually published with the briefer and to my mind inferior title of *Evening Light*.

If no one wanted it, that was OK. I'd self-publish, and lodge a few copies in the libraries. Meanwhile, I sent extracts to the literary journals, and six of them were published as short stories. I then gave the manuscript to Lesley Choyce, asking his opinion whether I should simply lodge it in the archives, and to my surprise he wanted to publish it. He did a handsome job, too, with iceberg photographs by Andrew on both covers. Some day this book will be republished, perhaps even in mass-market format.

Almost at the same time, Killick Press brought out the first volume of my memoirs, *A Walk in the Dreamtime*, beautifully produced and well-received, convincing me that I should continue with a final volume, *Among the Lions*.

At this time, too, I published ten copies of my long Labrador poem, *Cycle of the Sun*, which I had begun writing back in the 1950s. One bit of it—the spring section, which was the first written—had won the first poetry award offered by the Newfoundland Arts and Letters Competition. Over the years I had gone back to this cycle several times, making minor revisions. Then I did a major rewrite in 1994, and tried it out on a few friends with little response. So I published the ten-copy edition electronically in binders designed for students, and lodged them in the National Library, the Newfoundland Collection of Memorial University, and my own collection at the University of

Calgary. I believed that real poetry could rarely find a market nowadays, even when written in free verse form. There seemed to me no audience for anything that made prose sense and had poetic structure. I was amazed—almost shocked—when Newfoundland's literary magazine, *TickleAce*, paid me $340 for the poem. There must still be literate academics and editors out there, if you can find them.

I also wrote a true sonnet, in the strict Italian form, with the title, "A Sonnet for My Brother in His Sixty-Sixth Year." It appeared in *The Newfoundland Quarterly*, and was read at my brother's funeral. He died of lymphoma June 22, 1994, while Corky, Leah and I were crossing the continental divide by car on our way to the west coast of Vancouver Island. We learned of his death three days later when we visited a campsite on a river flat near Port Alberni.

Charlie and I had carried on a lively philosophical correspondence until a few months before his death. Among the things that lightened his last illness was a volume of notes on science and engineering that Andrew collected by shortwave radio from such sources as The Netherlands, Russia, India, China and Japan. When Charlie became too ill to read this material himself, John read it to him, and they discussed it together. He was sixty-nine.

A strict sonnet in the Italian manner is a very difficult poem to write in English. It took me more than two years to complete that one, through numerous starts and revisions. It was one of those poems that poets so often encounter—something that seemed to be there, simply waiting for the writer to "find" it. I finished the octet at least a year before I even started the sestet, and thought that the poem might never get any further than that. Then one day the sestet started to appear, almost fully developed. Poetry is often fashioned in the subconscious over a long period of gestation.

When it was finished, I felt like standing up and cheering. Here was a poem that wholly satisfied me, something by which I'd be willing to "stand or fall" as Conrad said. But how you get the anthologists to recognize a poem when one appears I haven't a clue. Perhaps, at some future time, someone will "find" this poem, and rescue it from oblivion. Perhaps, a year or two hence, I'll collect my few poems, including *Cycle of the Sun*, into a slim volume, which can then be buried in the doubtful and uncertain hope of resurrection. Canadian writing meanwhile will go its way into colloquialism and media-speak.

I've had a wonderful life. I've had the great privilege of visiting and enjoying many parts of the world from the tropics to the Arctic. Unlike the "snowbirds" who fly to a warm city and lie on a beach, gaining nothing more than a few degrees of temperature, I have been immersed in the world's wonders wherever I went, and especially in the miracle of life's unfolding. I've camped in every province of Canada, and in all of the "contiguous forty-eight" American states; I've visited Europe, Mexico, and the Caribbean, swum with manatees, waded with ibises and spoonbills, and everywhere found people, especially children, who were glad to become my instant friends.

This alone would have made life abundantly worthwhile, but I have also been privileged to live at a time when we have begun to understand at least a part of how it all came about, and the process by which it is proceeding. We are a long way from penetrating to the ultimate secret of how and why the universe we know began to evolve, and continued to become ever more complex and beautiful, but, unlike any people before us, we have been able to grasp some billions of years of the process—to understand the creation in a holistic if still incomplete fashion.

We see in part, as Saint Paul said in his first letter to the Corinthians, but the part that we see is so vast and intricate and complex as to be breathtaking. We have watched the hydrogen ions emerge from the primal fireball, the galaxies and the stars come to birth in numbers that are incomprehensible, across times and distances that no mind can grasp, worlds without number spinning into light from the darkness, life permeating it all, growing into ever more complex miracles, and our own small world groping its way toward an integrated civilization that may some day encompass the solar system.

"Bliss was it in that dawn to be alive," Wordsworth said in one of the very few memorable lines that he wrote. If it seemed to Wordsworth that the emergence of the bourgeois class in his time was a great dawn, how much more reason have we to rejoice in the dawn that now surrounds us—the dawn of daybreak through the gateways of the mind, seeing for the first time in human history, and in some detail, the miracle in which we are immersed, and of which we are a part. To be here at this moment when the human mind has begun to expand into the universe is a privilege beyond anything that earlier generations could have imagined.

—*HH. Annapolis Basin*
Nova Scotia, Canada
Year 1 of the 21st century.